Divorce in Ireland

MARITAL BREAKDOWN, ANSWERS AND ALTERNATIVES

To Moth
(Kieron Wood)

To my Mother
(Paul O'Shea)

Divorce in Ireland

MARITAL BREAKDOWN, ANSWERS AND
ALTERNATIVES

Kieron Wood B.L.

and

Paul O'Shea, Solicitor

FOREWORD BY

The Hon Mrs Justice Catherine McGuinness
Judge of the Supreme Court

Published in 2003 by
First Law Limited
Merchant's Court,
Merchants Quay,
Dublin 8,
Ireland.

Typeset by Gough Typesetting Services, Dublin.

ISBN 1-904480-047

A catalogue record for this book
is available from the British Library.

Printed by Johnswood Press Ltd, Dublin.

Foreword

In my Foreword to the first edition of this book I welcomed it as a timely contribution to public knowledge at the time when the Family Law (Divorce) Act 1996 was coming into force. The Law Reform Commission in its Report on *Family Courts* published in March 1996 (LRC52-1996) had pointed out that:

> "The last twenty years have seen a growing recognition by society of the wide variety of problems associated with the breakdown of family relationships. Substantive family law has undergone a transformation during this period, with the introduction of a wide range of remedies and rights designed to protect vulnerable or dependent family members in the wake of breakdown, and to secure the fair distribution of family assets."

The ending of the constitutional ban on divorce and the enactment of the Family Law (Divorce) Act 1996 marked a watershed in Irish family law. In the first edition of *Divorce in Ireland* the authors Kieron Wood and Paul O'Shea provided a wide ranging summary of remedies available to those suffering from the tragedy of marriage breakdown. The book was addressed to the interested general reader rather than to the legal specialist and in this way provided a most useful service.

In this second edition the authors have had the advantage of seeing the practical outcome of the provisions of the 1996 Act through the many cases that have come before the Courts.

In their comprehensive new chapter on divorce they point out that the number of applications for divorce have risen steadily, just over fifteen thousand applications having been received by the Courts up to the end of 2001. They acknowledge, however, that this is a considerably lower figure than was anticipated, at least by some, at the time of the Constitutional Referendum. The chapter outlines the major decisions which have been made by the Courts in this area — on the meaning of "living apart", on the enforcement of foreign maintenance orders, and on the division of assets where the financial resources of the couple are large. This survey includes an analysis of the most recent Supreme Court decision in *T. v. T.* (unreported, October 14, 2002).

In their preface, Mr Wood and Mr O'Shea draw attention to the need for changes in the law in a number of areas. They highlight the difficulties caused by the strict operation of the statutory *in camera* rule, which has led to problems both in the public perception of the operation of the Family Law Courts and in providing a method of reporting the legal aspects of decisions made by these Courts. In a welcome recent development both the Attorney General and the Minister for Justice, in the Programme for Government, forecast a general system of reporting which would continue to respect the privacy of litigants.

This new edition also draws attention to the effect of EU Council Regulation 1347 covering the recognition and enforcement of judgments in matrimonial matters. This Regulation, which became part of Irish law on March 1, 2001, is generally known as Brussels II, and has crucially changed the rules for recognition of foreign divorces within the European Union. It has been much criticised by family lawyers both in this country and in Britain as being an encouragement to "forum-shopping" and as putting a premium on the early issue of Court proceedings where settlement negotiations or mediation might provide a better solution to the problems of separating couples. At present negotiations are taking place at EU level for a further extension of this Regulation. It appears that moves are also taking place to develop a set of family law principles, which would apply in all of the Member States of the European Union. These developments will be of vital interest to all family law writers and practitioners.

As I commented in regard to the first edition, this book is to some extent aimed at the many people who are themselves experiencing marital difficulties and who are seeking basic information about the remedies open to them and the various paths they might follow. In this context the information given about counselling, mediation and legal aid is most important. The authors rightly note that the legislative provisions on mediation and counselling are not always fully reflected in family law practice and it is important that proper provision be made for these alternative solutions in our family law system.

Divorce in Ireland is not, of course, a substitute for full legal advice from practising family law solicitors and counsel. The authors themselves point this out by appending this advice to the list of contents at the beginning of the book and by adding the old adage that *"a person who represents himself in Court has a fool for a client."* Nevertheless this second edition again provides a useful, clear and informative introduction to the legislation and case law on divorce and related family law topics. Doubtless it will again have a wide readership.

Mrs. Justice Catherine McGuinness

November 2002

Preface

"Breaking up is hard to do," sang Neil Sedaka in 1962 – and he was right. Divorce is one of the most stressful experiences in life. According to the latest Review of the Registrar General in England and Wales, the death rate for divorced women aged over 25 is up to 58% higher than for married women. For divorced men, it's even worse, with death rates 70–100% higher than married men.

Divorce is an option that few people foresee or desire. Many people will go to great lengths to avoid a separation – though few go as far as retired Sicilian policeman Rosolino Daiello, who pulled out a gun and shot dead his wife at a judicial separation hearing in Milan in September 2002.

Most family law applications are brought by women, and there appears to be a growing feeling among men that the family law courts are biased against them. Accurate statistics are hard to come by because of the *in camera* rule, under which proceedings in the family court are heard in private and may not be reported.

Increasingly, there have been calls for a relaxation of the rule. Attorney General Rory Brady, addressing a family law conference in October 2002, said the process of examining the detailed effects of divorce in Ireland was hampered by the rule as it now stood. "Its application is absolute and this creates difficulties on a number of levels, including the handling of professional conduct complaints," he said. "I would welcome general reporting of these cases, carried out in a manner which protects absolutely the secrecy of the identity of the couple and the family."

Other difficulties in the practical implementation of family law statutes have also become apparent to practitioners over the past few years.

In 2002, the Supreme Court struck down a section of the 1996 Domestic Violence Act because it allowed a person to be barred from the family home for an unspecified period without having a chance to put his (or her) side of the story to the court. The government is likely to react by imposing a time limit for the hearing of the full barring application.

But there are other ways of ensuring justice – such as requiring that any *ex parte* barring application (based on the evidence of one side) should be based only on an affidavit, a sworn written statement.

This would ensure that the respondent was fully aware of the allegations which had to be rebutted, and it would prevent a situation where an applicant could make an emotional plea which might sway a judge in the absence of the respondent.

Another concern of the courts is "limping marriages" – that is, marriages which are recognised in one country but not another. This was a particular problem before the availability of divorce in Ireland.

However, it is still likely to trouble the courts in the future because of the disparity between the marriage age in the Ireland and the UK. Under the 1995 Family Law Act, if an 18-year-old youth who is resident in the Republic marries a 17-year-old Northern Ireland girl resident in the North (as might well happen in a cross-border parish), the marriage would be legal in the North, but void in the Republic. That situation should be addressed now, before it causes serious problems. Another matter which needs to be addressed is that of guardianship. Unmarried fathers may now become guardians of their children by making a joint sworn declaration with the child's mother. But the only record of that declaration is the document they have sworn, which could be lost or accidentally destroyed.

In circumstances where an unmarried father is a guardian

and chooses to appoint a testamentary guardian in his will, the validity of that decision can only be proved if the declaration can be found after his death. There should be a national guardianship register in which such declarations can be formally recorded.

In relation to divorce, pre-nuptial agreements remain contrary to public policy. The effect of this can sometimes be to prevent couples marrying – particularly where one partner may have had a previous unhappy marital experience and does not wish to risk losing everything a second time. As a result, children (and partners) may be deprived of the right to a stable home, with the constitutional protection afforded only to married couples.

The *Civitas Report*, published in the UK in 2002, reported that the increased rate of cohabitation, both for first-time partnerships and for new partnerships, had been linked in part to a desire to avoid divorce by having a 'trial' marriage or by avoiding legal ties altogether.

It is time for the government to realise that marriages do break down, and to allow couples (following independent legal advice) to decide for themselves how they wish to regulate their families and their finances for the future.

The government should also be doing what it can to preserve faltering marriages. Section 6 of the Divorce Act specified that "the minister may make regulations to allow for the establishment of a register of professional organisations whose members are qualified to assist the parties involved in effecting a reconciliation."

This commendable proposal has never been put into effect. If the government is serious about trying to protect the family and avoid marriage breakdown, it should make the required regulations forthwith.

Kieron Wood, Barrister at Law
Paul O'Shea, Solicitor,
November 2002

Table of Contents

IMPORTANT: This book is not a substitute for the advice of an experienced family law solicitor. Remember, a person who represents himself in court has a fool for a client!

Chapter One

Family Law in Ireland

Until the end of the Middle Ages, Irish couples in failed marriages could divorce by mutual consent. A woman might divorce her husband for being sterile, gossiping about their marital relations, failing to maintain her or beating her. A husband could divorce his wife for bad housekeeping, persistent illness, barrenness or if he wanted to go on a pilgrimage or become a monk.

Gradually, Christian teaching on the indissolubility of marriage spread throughout Europe. But, in recent times, Christian rules have been increasingly ignored and marital breakdown has become more widespread. Most countries have now legislated for civil divorce.

In 1995, Ireland was the only country in the European Union to forbid civil divorce. Article 41.3.2° of the 1937 Irish Constitution said: "No law shall be enacted providing for the grant of a dissolution of marriage."

The ban reflected the Catholic views of the vast majority of the people – and the judiciary – of the Irish Republic.

Even as late as the 1950s, there was strong public opposition to divorce. In 1958, a woman who had already obtained an English divorce sued her ex-husband in the Irish courts to recover £339.1s.5d in legal costs awarded by the English court.

Irish courts will normally enforce a valid foreign court judgment but, in this instance, the Supreme Court said that the Irish judiciary "would fail to carry out public policy if, by a decree of its own courts, it gave assistance to the process of divorce by entertaining a suit for the costs of such proceedings."

By 1962, however, attitudes in society had begun to change. When the High Court refused an order for the examination of an Irish witness in a foreign divorce case, the Minister for External Affairs appealed to the Supreme Court, which granted the application.

In 1978, a woman who had obtained a divorce in England applied to the Irish High Court for the enforcement of a maintenance order. The judge said that providing maintenance for a spouse did not give active assistance to the process of divorce, so could not be regarded as contrary to public policy.

In 1986, the Irish government tried to remove the ban on divorce, but the electorate rejected the proposals by a majority of almost two to one (935,843 votes to 538,279). The defeat at that time was put down to the influence of the Catholic Church and the fear of farmers and house owners that divorce would affect their property rights.

The following year, in the case of *Johnston v. Ireland*, a couple complained to the European Court that the Constitutional ban on divorce was a breach of their human rights.

But the Court of Human Rights in Strasbourg held that the guarantee of the right to marry in the European Convention on Human Rights did not imply an equal right to divorce. The Court also said that Article 8 of the Convention, on the respect due to family life, did not require Ireland to introduce divorce.

Pro-divorce campaigners pressed for another vote. The second referendum, in 1995, proposed to replace Article 41.3.2° with the formula:

> "A court designated by law may grant a dissolution of marriage where, but only where, it is satisfied that:
> (i)   at the date of the institution of proceedings, the spouses have lived apart from one another for a period of, or periods amounting to, at least four years during the preceding five years,

(ii) there is no reasonable prospect of reconciliation between the spouses,

(iii) such provision as the court considers proper having regard to the circumstances, exists or will be made for the spouses, any children of either or both of them and any other person prescribed by law, and

(iv) any further conditions prescribed by law are complied with."

In the period leading up to the second referendum, successive governments enacted extensive legislation to deal with property rights. The major piece of legislation was the 1989 Judicial Separation and Family Law Reform Act, which was substantially amended by the 1995 Family Law Act.

In 1986, the influence of the Catholic Church had been pivotal in defeating the divorce proposals, but by 1995, things were different. A series of scandals had rocked the Church and trust in Church leaders was at an all-time low.

As the campaign reached its peak, Mother Teresa of Calcutta and Pope John Paul II urged the Irish electorate to consider the sacredness of marriage and vote against divorce. But their voices went unheard.

The result of the poll could hardly have been closer. At the final count, the electorate had voted in favour of divorce by 818,842 votes to 809,728. The majority – slightly over 9,000 votes in a poll of 1.6 million – amounted to just over half of one %.

A divisional High Court rejected a legal challenge to the result by anti-divorce campaigners, ruling that the court could not interfere with the democratic process.

Five Supreme Court judges unanimously rejected an appeal. They criticised the government's "unconstitutional and anti-democratic" decision to spend half a million pounds promoting a *Yes* vote, but said there was no proof that the campaign had materially affected the outcome of the poll.

After the judgment, the Catholic Bishops issued a statement reminding Catholics that Church teaching on the indissolubility of marriage had not changed. They said the valid and consummated marriage of a baptised man and woman absolutely excluded marriage to anyone else while both spouses were still alive.

In the event, the expected rush for divorces never materialised. Claims that 80,000 people were in broken marriages and just waiting to divorce proved to be gross exaggerations. Between February 27, 1997 (when the Divorce Act came into force) and December 31, 2001, 10,182 divorces were granted in the Circuit Court, with a further 83 in the High Court.

Unhappily, the introduction of divorce has not contributed to the stability of marriage in Ireland. Five years after divorce became available, the increasing incidence of marriage breakdown is reflected in the growing number of court applications in family law matters. Between 1990 and 2000, the number of District Court applications rose from 8,028 to 23,452 – almost a threefold increase.

The number might have been even greater except for the fact that the number of marriages is falling. In the Republic of Ireland, the total number of people getting married fell from a high of 22,180 couples in 1980 to 17,360 in 1995.

Today, a divorce may be obtained more easily than ever. Under a European Directive, a divorce obtained in any other EU country (except Denmark) will be recognised in Ireland. This appears to have undermined the requirement in Irish law for a four-year separation.

The Irish courts have ruled that separation does not necessarily mean living in separate houses and, in the case of *T. v. T.* (2002), the Chief Justice hinted that "clean break" divorces were now a real possibility.

Divorce has now become an accepted part of life in 21st century Ireland.

Chapter Two

Options

Marriage is one of the social institutions, which helps hold society together. Marriage breakdown is a tragedy for all concerned: the couple, any children and society as a whole.

Most marriages go through a difficult period at one time or another, but that does not mean that couples should separate at the first cross word.

The aim of this book is not to encourage separation or divorce. Where a relationship is worth saving, couples should work at resolving their differences. Whatever the difficulties – financial problems, infidelity, alcohol, gambling, drugs, and sexual incompatibility – there are organisations that can probably help. Many of them are listed on page 259 at the end of this book.

Couples with children should make a particular effort to overcome their difficulties through counselling, as the effect of separation or divorce on children can be traumatic and may last a lifetime, even affecting the children's own future relationships. In one study cited in the *Civitas Report* in 2002, 64% of unhappy couples who stayed together and worked on their relationship, reported being happy five years later.

But, if after undergoing counselling, a couple still decide to part company, they should carefully consider a wide range of important options.

The first thing they should realise is that, if they were married in church, there are two elements to the marriage: civil and religious. For many couples, the main consideration is their legal or contractual relationship, brought about by a valid civil marriage. For others, the religious aspect of marriage is more important.

In relation to the civil contract, there are three possible avenues for couples who choose to split up: nullity, separation or divorce.

If there were no valid marriage from the start, either spouse would be entitled to apply for a decree of nullity – even if the couple had been together for many years and had a large family.

If there *was* a valid civil marriage, the two options are separation (in which case neither partner may remarry) or divorce (after which remarriage is permitted).

In relation to the religious aspect of marriage, although all the main Christian Churches claim to regard marriage as a divine life-long institution, all except the Catholic Church permit the remarriage of divorced people in church.

Non-Catholics, therefore, may divorce and remarry in church without any difficulty. Catholics who have been validly married may not remarry in church unless their spouse dies. Catholics who wish to marry a new partner in church while the first partner is still alive must first be granted an ecclesiastical (or Church) nullity, which is a ruling by the Church authorities that the earlier supposed "marriage" never existed.

So the first issue to be addressed by any couple wishing to separate has to be: were we really married?

That may seem an odd question to ask, particularly if the couple went through a marriage ceremony, have been together for many years and perhaps have several children. But it's not as straightforward as that. There may be a number of reasons why the marriage was void from the beginning – perhaps because of a problem with the ceremony or with the couple themselves.

If there is any doubt about the validity of a marriage, either partner should consult an experienced family law solicitor who will explain the grounds for a civil declaration of nullity.

If the couple discover that they are not married, that has

wide-ranging implications for them. Clearly either partner may marry, as the first "marriage" was not valid. They may not avail of Constitutional or legislative protection for the family, as they are not husband and wife. Their children, while not illegitimate, become "non-marital" children. Any agreement entered into on the basis that they were married (such as a separation agreement) would be null and void.

If a couple do decide to seek a civil nullity, they may decide – at any time – to validate their marriage, if it is possible to do so. If, for example, one of the partners was under age at the time of the "marriage", the couple may choose to re-marry one another (assuming that both parties are over 18 at the time of that decision).

If there is no doubt about the validity of the marriage, and the couple want to split up formally without recourse to the courts (and do not wish to marry someone else), the simplest solution is probably a separation agreement. Such an agreement may be negotiated even before the couple separate and no statutory pre-conditions are required.

Separation agreements are private contracts. Before the Reformation, they were illegal, but they are now accepted as a way of allowing a couple to make their own arrangements for separation without the necessity for a court battle. (Pre-nuptial agreements, however, are still not permitted, as the courts consider they may destabilise the marriage contract.)

Separation agreements must be drawn up *voluntarily* and may be set aside if there is any suggestion of duress, undue influence or misrepresentation. The agreement – which ends the duty to cohabit – should be drawn up with the benefit of legal advice.

In *V.W. v. J.W.* (1978), the judge refused to set aside an agreement where the wife deliberately did not seek legal advice because, she claimed, she was an alcoholic. (Initials are normally used in reports of family law cases, in order to protect the anonymity of those involved.)

Most issues can be resolved in the separation agreement,

though the law does not permit a spouse to contract out of future maintenance payments. The 1964 Guardianship of Infants Act allows parents to specify in a separation agreement who should have custody of the children.

After the agreement has been drawn up, it may be "ruled" by the court, giving it the force of a court order.

The courts will not look favourably on anyone who – after proper advice – freely enters into a separation agreement, and later tries to wriggle out of it. In *Hyman v. Hyman* (1929), the court said a separation agreement should be drawn up, construed, dissolved and enforced on exactly the same principles as any other commercial agreement.

But the court may vary a separation agreement, if there are substantial changes in a person's circumstances. In *M.G. v. M.G.* (2000), a couple had signed a separation agreement in which the husband had agreed to transfer his interest in the family home to the wife in return for a payment of £20,000. The house was then worth £200,000.

Later, the husband lost his job and asked the court to vary the original agreement. At that stage, the family home was valued at £800,000. The judge said:

> "Where the parties are well-educated intelligent persons who have had the benefit of competent legal advice before entering into a recent separation agreement, it seems to me that the court should be slow to make any radical alterations to the terms of such agreement unless there have been sufficient changes in the situations of the parties.
>
> "Making any significant alterations to the arrangements may well cause further distress to the children, who may well see themselves as vulnerable pawns in a renewed conflict between their parents."

But the judge said that, if the couple could have foreseen the "remarkable increase in residential property values", he doubted whether the husband would have "so readily surrendered all his interest in the family home."

The judge ruled that the husband should continue to pay maintenance but should receive 10% of the proceeds of any future sale of the family home – though he was not to have any equitable right to the property.

If a separating couple disagree about ownership of property, the court may decide the issue under the 1957 Married Women's Status Act. A claim under the 1957 Act is not like a claim to a property adjustment order under the Judicial Separation, Family Law or Divorce Acts, where the court takes many more factors into consideration.

For a spouse to be entitled to some share in the other spouse's property, there must have been some direct or indirect financial contribution.

Mr Justice Tom Finlay said in *W. v. W.* (1981) that:

> "Where a wife contributes by money to the purchase of a property by her husband in his sole name, in the absence of evidence of some inconsistent agreement or arrangement, the court will decide that the wife is entitled to an equitable interest in that property approximately proportionate to the extent of her contribution ...

> "Where a wife contributes either directly towards the repayment of mortgage instalments or contributes to a general family fund, thus releasing her husband from an obligation which he otherwise would have to discharge liabilities out of that fund and permitting him to repay mortgage instalments, she will – in the absence of proof of an inconsistent agreement or arrangement – be entitled to an equitable share in the property – approximately proportionate to her contribution.

"Where a wife expends monies or carries out work in the improvement of a property which has been originally acquired by – and the legal ownership in which is solely in – her husband, she will have no claim in respect of such contributions unless she established by evidence that, from the circumstances surrounding the making of it, she was led to believe – or, of course, that it was specifically agreed – that she would be recompensed for it. Even where such a right to recompense is established – either by an express agreement or by circumstances in which the wife making the contribution was led to such belief – it is a right to recompense in monies only and cannot and does not constitute a right to claim an equitable share in the estate of the property concerned."

In *McC. v. McC.* (1986) Henchy J. said that:

"When the wife's contribution has been indirect (such as contributing, by means of her earnings, to a general family fund), the court will – in the absence of any express or implied agreement to the contrary – infer a trust in favour of the wife, on the grounds that she has to that extent relieved the husband of the financial burden he incurred in purchasing the house."

In *C.D. v. W.D. and Barclays Bank* (1997), C.D. claimed a beneficial interest in a 26-acre County Kilkenny farm, which was held in her husband's sole name. The husband, W.D., had been full owner of the lands since 1972, 11 years before the couple married. In 1989, Barclays Bank registered a charge over the land (which did not include the family home).

The wife, who was a nurse, said she had contributed about £25,000 towards the building of the family home in County Laois, which was also held in the husband's sole name. She also used her income to pay day-to-day household expenses.

She said that her husband had promised to put the Kilkenny land into their joint names, though nothing was ever done.

The bank obtained an order for possession in 1991 and served all the papers on the wife, but she made no claim to the land before the issue of the 1995 proceedings. She said she was unaware that she had any rights, but the judge said that was not the attitude of a joint owner.

The judge said the wife's action was "more a last ditch effort to rescue some form of asset from the bank than a true dispute between herself and her husband."

Although the wife had made a substantial direct contribution to the family home, she did not make any claim to a share in the house. Her claim applied only to the Kilkenny land, towards which she had made no direct contribution.

The court ruled that her indirect contribution to the "general family fund" could not have given her any interest in the Kilkenny land between the marriage in 1983 and the bank's charge in 1986, since the husband was already the full owner.

The main matters dealt with by a separation agreement are:

• the agreement to live separately,

• a "non-molestation" clause, which means each spouses will not interfere in the life of the other,

• arrangements for children, including custody, access, holidays and foreign travel,

• future ownership of any property,

• maintenance and lump sum payments,

• indemnity from the debts of the other spouse,

• taxable status, and

• succession rights.

Sadly, not all couples are willing to negotiate separation terms amicably. The anguish, which frequently accompanies the end of a relationship, can lead to anger, vindictiveness and a desire to "pay back" the other partner. In such circumstances, it may be impossible for the spouses to negotiate an agreement. The remaining alternatives are usually either judicial separation or divorce.

A decree of judicial separation does not give a right to remarry – merely to live apart. The couple remain married, so if both partners subsequently decide to give the relationship another chance, they may resume living together without the necessity for a remarriage (and without necessarily returning to court).

Until 1997, when divorce became available in Ireland, the only way to end a valid civil marriage finally and irrevocably was to establish a domicile abroad and obtain a divorce there. While this may have been an option for couples with no family ties in Ireland, it was not a realistic possibility for most people.

Even where one partner did obtain a foreign divorce, the decree might not always be recognised in Ireland because of problems of domicile. Until 1986, a foreign divorce would only be recognised in Ireland if granted in the country where both spouses were domiciled (not just resident).

The Oireachtas abolished the dependent domicile rule and amended the divorce recognition rule in the 1986 Domicile and Recognition of Foreign Divorces Act which says that a divorce will now be recognised if granted in the country where *either* spouse is domiciled.

In *C.M. v. T.M. (No. 2)* (1990), the High Court held that the common law rule that a married woman's domicile depended on that of her husband had been swept away by principles of equality before the law and equal rights in marriage enshrined in the Constitution. This decision was upheld by the Supreme Court in *W. v. W.* (1993).

But the problem of recognition continues to be an issue

for the courts. For example, in *P.K. (orse C.) v. T.K.* (2002), an Irish husband and his American wife had married in New York in 1963 then moved to Ireland. In 1977, the marriage broke down and the wife returned to New York, leaving the children with the husband in Ireland. The husband obtained an uncontested divorce in New York in 1980. The wife did not seek any maintenance.

Twenty years later, the wife sought a divorce in Ireland, claiming that the New York divorce was invalid because neither spouse was domiciled in New York at the time. She maintained that she had only lived in New York because of economic necessity and had always intended to return to Ireland.

The High Court ruled that the husband's domicile was New York State, so the decree of the New York court would be recognised in Ireland and the couple were not married here. The wife appealed the decision.

The Supreme Court said it was clear that the wife wanted an Irish divorce so she could seek maintenance. But the court said the overwhelming evidence was that the wife had either reverted to her domicile of origin or had chosen New York as a domicile of choice by living there for 22 years.

Under the 1996 Divorce Act, when the courts grant a divorce, the valid, subsisting civil marriage is dissolved. If the man and woman later decide they want to live together again as husband and wife, they will have to go through the whole marriage procedure again.

Chapter Three

Mediation and Counselling

No couple should put an end to their marriage without first trying to salvage the partnership. That particularly applies where there are children, who may be severely psychologically and emotionally traumatised by the breakdown of their parents' relationship. Counselling services exist throughout Ireland to help couples who want to try and resolve their difficulties with the aim of staying together.

Accord (formerly the *Catholic Marriage Advisory Council*) provides a confidential service to help clients resolve conflict and difficulties in their relationships. The counsellors listen to the couple, separately and eventually together, and discuss their problems in a non-directive and non-confrontational way to enable them to make their own decisions.

Couples who may have sexual problems in their marriages, who wish to decide the size of their family or who encounter difficulties in having children, may use *Accord*'s marital sex therapy or fertility management services. Marriage preparation courses cover various areas of the marital relationship, including communication, sexuality, family planning, children, conflict resolution and marital spirituality.

Accord currently has 743 counsellors and facilitators providing marriage and relationship counselling services in 57 centres nationwide. Marital sex therapy is offered in 12 centres.

In 2001, 5,425 people used the marriage counselling service, involving 25,828 hours of counselling. Demand for marriage preparation courses often exceeds availability, with

10,877 people attending the courses in 2001. During 2000, the 123 Dublin counsellors gave 12,000 hours of counselling to more than 3,000 people. Of those, 40% had been married for less than 10 years, just over half from 11 to 30 years and almost 10% had been married for over 30 years.

The main complaint was about poor communication between partners, followed by domestic violence and depression. Family issues were often an underlying problem and about 10% of couples cited infidelity as the reason for coming to *Accord*.

As a result of the introduction of reception interviews and the payment of counsellors, waiting lists are now much shorter and new clients are likely to be seen within two weeks at any centre.

Counselling services are free for those who cannot afford to pay, but clients are generally expected to make a contribution in accordance with guidelines given at the reception interview. In 2000, clients donated an average of €5.61 an hour. Counselling services are also available throughout the country for those of other religions (or none). Addresses of counselling services can be found on page 260.

But if reconciliation is not an option and a couple have irrevocably decided to go their separate ways, they should be advised to consider mediation before turning to the courts.

The *Family Mediation Service* offers separating couples (or couples who have already separated) the opportunity to negotiate their *own* agreements with the help of a mediator. The service was set up in 1986 as a pilot service. It was placed on a permanent footing in 1993 and is now under the auspices of the Department of Social, Community and Family Affairs. There are offices in Dublin, Marino, Tallaght, Cork, Limerick, Galway, Athlone, Dundalk, Tralee, Wexford and Castlebar.

The professional, confidential service is free and is available to married and non-married couples. It is not marriage counselling nor a legal advice centre. The underlying principle is that couples solve their own problems with the assistance of a professionally-trained mediator, rather than have decisions made for them by someone else.

Mediation can only work if both parties freely agree to try it. Any legal proceedings that may already have been issued must be adjourned or suspended for six months. Successful mediation is likely to take between two and six one-hour sessions.

All issues are open to negotiation, including child custody and access, living arrangements, the family home, financial support, property, education and health. Both sides must make a full and frank disclosure of any relevant information at mediation if the process is to be successful.

All discussions are confidential and the mediator will not discuss the case with anyone else. The mediator is neutral, does not take sides and will not voluntarily testify in court on behalf of either party. Under the Divorce Act, neither spouse will be allowed to produce in evidence any matters discussed or written down during an attempted reconciliation or mediation.

Either party (or the mediator) may withdraw from the discussions at any time. If agreement is reached, the parties are advised to have the agreement checked by their solicitors. The mediation document is not legally binding on the parties, but frequently forms the basis for a formal separation agreement, which can be drawn up by the couple's solicitors.

In the first session, the mediator discusses the couple's decision to separate. They are asked why they have come to mediation and what their expectations are. Most couples want to mediate four main issues: children, the family home, finances and property. Others have already agreed some issues and want to mediate the remainder. If money is an issue, the couple are given budget forms to complete for a session on finances.

The next stage of mediation is exploration of the issues and the development of options. One issue at a time is dealt with: finance, then property, and then children. The couple are asked to develop different options to meet their perceived needs. They are asked to choose their preferred option and keep it under consideration until the final session on negotiation and decision-making. In the meantime, both parties will probably consult a solicitor and an auctioneer, who can value the family home.

Finally, the mediator will produce a written agreement setting out the intentions and decisions of the couple. The document may be modified after further consideration or after either side has consulted a solicitor. If the final document is perceived to be illegal, unfair to one partner or drawn up in bad faith, the mediator may withdraw from mediation.

Having come to an agreement, the couple are invited to bring in their children for a joint session, explaining that they intend to split up as husband and wife, but remain jointly as parents of the children. They may invite suggestions from older children in relation to the parenting plan. Six months after the final session, a review session is held to discuss how the agreement has worked and consider any necessary changes.

Seven leaflets are available to help separating couples deal with all aspects of separation, including dealing with feelings of grief, loss and anger that many couples experience, the reactions of children to the separation of their parents and the question of what separating couples should tell their children.

Mediation services are also available from *Gingerbread Ireland*. The organisation, which also offers counselling and legal advice for lone parents, has branches in Dublin, Blanchardstown, Wexford, Cork, Limerick and Drogheda. Membership is open to people who are bringing up children on their own. Gingerbread runs free courses on subjects including self-esteem, conflict-handling and parenting, and organises lectures and advice on a wide variety of topics of interest to lone parents.

Chapter Four

Domestic Violence

The breakdown of a marriage is not infrequently accompanied by ill-feeling to the point of mental cruelty, threats or even violence. Historically, a spouse (usually a wife) whose husband owned the family home had to suffer his behaviour, or else leave home. Changing attitudes in society led to amendment of the law to protect spouses, partners, parents and children.

Four types of court order may now be obtained to protect a spouse, dependent child or "persons in other domestic relationships." The person who applies for such an order is known as the applicant. The person against whom the order is directed is the respondent.

A *safety order* prevents the respondent using (or threatening to use) violence against the applicant – or molesting or frightening that person. If the applicant and respondent do not live in the same house, the safety order also prevents the respondent from "watching or besetting" the place where the applicant lives. If they *do* live in the same house, the respondent does not have to leave.

A *protection order* is an interim (temporary) order, which has the same effect as a safety order.

A *barring order* has a similar effect to a safety order, except that it prevents the respondent using (or threatening to use) violence against the applicant or *any* dependent person and requires the respondent to leave home and not to re-enter the property. Other conditions may be attached to the order.

An *interim barring order* may be made where there is an *immediate* risk of *significant* harm to the applicant or a dependent person and a protection order would be insufficient to protect the applicant. It has the same effect as a barring order and ceases to have effect when the court decides the barring order application.

Since 1976, the courts have been able to grant a barring order if required for the "safety or welfare" of either spouse or any dependent child under section 22 of the 1976 Family Law (Maintenance of Spouses and Children) Act. The term "welfare" includes physical and psychological welfare. The order required the offending spouse to leave a particular place (normally the family home) and not to re-enter it until further order of the court. The maximum penalty for a breach of the order was a £200 fine, six months' imprisonment or both.

The District Court could formerly only make a barring order for three months at a time. It could discharge the order if satisfied that the safety and welfare of the spouse and any children would not be prejudiced.

The 1976 Act was updated and extended by the 1981 Family Law (Protection of Spouses and Children) Act. That Act *only* applied to spouses and children, and did not extend to other family members or non-marital couples, such as so-called "common-law spouses."

The District Court could grant a *protection order* pending a barring order, preventing the respondent from using (or threatening to use) violence against the applicant, or molesting or frightening her. A barring order, if granted, lasted for up to one year and could only be renewed if there was evidence of further violence or threats.

The 1981 Act has now been replaced by the 1996 Domestic Violence Act, which also allows health boards to apply for orders. The Act extends the provision of safety, protection, interim barring and barring orders beyond spouses and children under 18 to "persons in other domestic relationships."

Applications may be made to the District or Circuit Court and will be heard informally in private. If necessary, the applicant may apply to the District Court for a protection order without notifying the other spouse. The District Judge must be given brief details of any threats, violence or mental cruelty.

If the order is granted, the judge will set a date for the hearing of a barring order application, when the other spouse may be represented. The protection order is sent to the local Garda station and, if any further incidents occur, the gardaí may take action. Those who can apply for orders include:

(1) the respondent's spouse,

(2) a person who has lived as husband and wife with the respondent for at least *six* months in the past year,

(3) the parent of an adult respondent,

(4) an adult who lives with the respondent in a non-contractual relationship (i.e. not a lodger, tenant or employee) or

(5) health boards.

A *safety order* may only be granted where required for the safety or welfare of the applicant or a dependant. The order prevents the respondent using or threatening to use violence against – or molesting or frightening – the applicant. If the couple do not live together, the respondent is also forbidden to "watch or beset" the place where the applicant lives. A District Court order lasts for up to five years and is renewable. The Circuit Court can make a safety order for an unlimited period.

In the case of a barring order, the applicant may be

(1) the respondent's spouse,

(2) a person who has lived with the respondent as husband and wife for at least *six* of the past *nine* months,

(3) the parent of an adult respondent or

(4) a health board.

The court will not make an order barring a person from his own home where a "common-law spouse" or parent has a lesser interest in the property.

The District Court may order the respondent to leave the family home and not to re-enter it for up to three years, and may renew the order thereafter for up to three years at a time if the applicant's welfare or safety requires. A Circuit Court order may be made without any time limit.

The order may also bar the respondent from using or threatening violence, molesting or frightening the applicant or any child or going anywhere near the applicant's home. Before granting the order, the court has to take into consideration the safety and welfare of any of the *respondent's* children who live in the family home.

Until a court finally decides whether or not to grant a barring or safety order, a spouse is not permitted to remove or dispose of any household goods. This requirement under the 1996 Act *only* applies to spouses.

If – after an application has been made for a barring order – a court believes there is an *immediate* risk that the applicant or her child will suffer "significant harm", it may make an *interim barring order* requiring the respondent to leave the applicant's home and stay away. In many cases, an interim barring order may be granted *ex parte*, that is without the respondent's knowledge and after having heard evidence from the applicant only. An interim order ceases to have effect when the court makes its decision on the full barring application.

Interim barring orders should only be granted in very limited circumstances, yet the statistics show that, of the 1,159 applications in 2001, 87% were granted.

Because the matters are heard *in camera*, details of the applications are not available to the public or to the legal profession. However, the background to one application came out in a judicial review application, which reached the Supreme Court in October 2002.

On November 6, 1998, Judge Timothy Crowley granted L.K. an interim barring order against her husband D.K. on an *ex parte* application. D.K. sought a declaration that the 1996 Act was unconstitutional, and he was given leave to apply for judicial review of the interim barring order.

In June 2000, Mr Justice Peter Kelly in the High Court refused to grant the reliefs sought on the basis that D.K. had not gone ahead with a District Court application to discharge the interim barring order.

The court heard that D.K. and L.K. were married in 1991 and had a daughter. The wife also had a son from a previous relationship who was adopted by D.K.

In her application for the interim barring order, the wife said:

> "For about the last year and a half, my husband has been physically and verbally abusive to me. He has a drink problem. He has hit me and pulled me around by the hair. He has smashed ornaments and articles. The children have witnessed this. Last night he came home drunk. I went down to my friend. The kids were with him.

> "He did not like this and began shouting at me, the children and the neighbours. I called the gardaí. He wouldn't give me my children. I had to stay in my friend's. This morning the lock was changed and he was gone with the children. Similar occurrences happen on a weekly basis. I am under stress and in fear and am seeking an interim barring order."

In his own affidavit, the husband said he was "most distressed" at the contents of the affidavit which, he said, were "largely untrue."

Senior counsel for the father said the 1996 Act deprived him of his right to be present in court to hear the allegations made against him and to confront or cross-examine his wife about her accusations. He said penalties for breach of an interim barring order were significantly more draconian than those that resulted from a breach of civil orders generally, involving a sentence of twelve months imprisonment and/or a fine of £1,500 (€1,905).

The Act expressly permitted an *ex parte* application that had the effect of removing the applicant against his will from the family home and the society of his child in proceedings where he was not heard by the court and had no opportunity of protecting his rights.

Counsel said an interim barring order could last for an unspecified period of time, in contrast to the provisions of the 1991 Child Care Act, under which a "fit person" order depriving a parent of the custody of a child could not last for more than eight days. (That was increased to 28 days by section 267(1)(a) of the 2001 Children Act.).

Unlike normal injunctions in civil proceedings, the interim barring order was mandatory, deprived the applicant – without any hearing – of his constitutional right to occupy the family home and rendered him guilty of a criminal offence if he didn't comply with the order.

Senior counsel for the State, said the 1996 Act was a necessary and reasonable legislative response to an accepted and pressing social need.

The Chief Justice said the Oireachtas could limit the constitutional right to due process in order to uphold other constitutional rights, but the extent of that restriction must be no more than was reasonably required to secure protection of the constitutional right in question. Chief Justice Keane said:

> "In the present case, it results in the forcible removal of the applicant from the family home and the society

of his child, on the basis of allegations in respect of which he has no opportunity of being heard, treats him as having committed a criminal offence resulting in a possible custodial sentence in the event of his non-compliance with the order and makes him liable to arrest by a garda without a warrant if the latter entertains a reasonable suspicion that he has failed to comply with the order."

"That the legislature were entitled to effect such an abridgement of the rights of individual citizens in order to deal with the social evil of domestic violence is beyond dispute. The question for resolution in this case is as to whether the manner in which the abridgement of the right to be heard has been effected is proportionate."

"Even where the District Court or the Circuit Court concludes that the interim order should never have been granted, it can do no more than discharge the order. The applicant cannot be required to compensate the respondent in any way for an order, which may have had the most damaging consequences for him.

"An interim barring order will typically be granted in a case where the relationship between the parties has effectively broken down and disputes have arisen, or will arise, in relation to matters such as custody of children, the payment of maintenance and adjustment of property rights. The granting of an interim order in the absence of the defendant may in such cases crucially tilt the balance of the entire litigation against him or her, to an extent, which may subsequently be difficult to redress.

"The failure of the legislation to impose any time limit on the operation of an interim barring order – is inexplicable.

"The District Court is a busy court of summary jurisdiction which deals with a huge volume of litigation and it may simply not be practicable to find a day for the hearing of the substantive barring order – as distinct from an interim order – until, as in the present case, a period of some months has elapsed."

"The procedures prescribed by subsection (1), (3) and (4) of [section 4 of] the 1996 Act, in failing to prescribe a fixed period of relatively short duration during which an interim barring order made *ex parte* is to continue in force, deprive the respondents to such applications of the protection of the principle of *audi alteram partem* [hear the other side] in a manner and to an extent which is disproportionate, unreasonable and unnecessary. The appeal will accordingly be allowed."

The court declared section 4(3) of the 1996 Act to be unconstitutional and it quashed the interim barring order. At the time of writing, the Government was expected to introduce a time limit for the hearing of full barring applications with evidence from both sides.

At a less drastic level than barring, the court may make a *protection* order before making a decision on either a barring or safety order. A protection order has the same effect as a safety order and ceases to have effect when the court makes its decision about the *barring* or *safety order*. In the case of a protection order, the respondent spouse is not barred from the family home.

If someone is too frightened to apply for a safety or barring order, a health board may do it on his or her behalf, but only if the board becomes aware of an incident which threatens a person's safety or welfare. The board must have reason to believe the "aggrieved person" is frightened for his or her safety or has been molested or subjected to threats or violence.

The health board has to take into account the wishes of

the aggrieved person "as far as is reasonably practicable." Clearly this section could give a health board power to interfere in a family relationship where neither partner wished the board to do so. Whether such a "bystanders' charter" would withstand a Constitutional challenge is open to question.

Any order is effective once the respondent has been told about it verbally and shown a copy of the order. Anyone who breaks a safety, barring, interim or protection order under the 1996 Act may be arrested without warrant and fined up to €1,905 or jailed for up to one year (or both).

If the respondent appeals against the order, the court can suspend the operation of a barring or safety order, but not a protection or interim barring order.

Where anyone (except a health board) applies for an order under the 1996 Act and it appears that a child care or supervision order might be necessary, the court may adjourn the proceedings and order the health board to investigate and report back to the court. In the meantime, the court may make such order as it sees fit under the 1991 Child Care Act for the care and custody of the child.

The court may also make orders relating to maintenance of a spouse and children, custody and access, child care, a child's birth or funeral expenses, protection of the family home and compensation for the loss of the home – even if proceedings have not been instituted under these headings.

The number of barring orders granted by the District Court has stayed fairly static since the enactment of the Domestic Violence Act. In 1996, 2,059 barring orders were granted. This rose to 2,319 in 2000, but fell back to just 2,067 in 2001. Similarly, the number of protection orders only rose from 3,521 in 1996 to 3,711 in 2001.

The two areas, which showed huge increases, were safety orders and interim barring orders. The number of safety orders granted by the District Court rose from 188 in 1996 to 1,232 in 2001. Interim barring orders showed a similar increase, with the number rising from 170 in 1996 to 1,007 in 2001 – a six-fold increase.

In cases where an applicant may not come within the requirements of the 1996 Domestic Violence Act – such as where the parties are not married and have not been living together for six months – relief may be sought under the 1997 Non-Fatal Offences Against the Person Act.

The Act says that it is an offence to threaten to kill or cause serious harm to a person or their children, to harass a person or to intimidate them into doing something or not doing something. Complaints should be made directly to the gardaí. A person convicted of a breach of the Act may be fined or jailed, and the court can order him or her not to communicate with the victim in future.

Chapter Five

Marriage Regulations

The first matter a solicitor will consider if a client is seeking a divorce or separation is whether the client was legally married in the first place. If not, clearly he or she will not require a divorce. It is important for the solicitor to find out whether the couple complied with the regulations when they married. If they did not, there is a possibility that the marriage may be null and void.

Marriage by civil ceremony is a civil contract. Marriage by certain religious denominations is also recognised in civil law as being a civil contract. For a marriage to be valid, the man and woman must be free to marry, they must have the required physical and psychological ability to "enter into and sustain a normal marital relationship" and they must marry voluntarily. Even if these conditions are fulfilled, they may still fall foul of regulations relating to age, notice, residency or other requirements, the absence of which may invalidate the marriage.

Both parties to a civil marriage in the Republic of Ireland must be over 18 years old on the day of the marriage. They must also have given three months' prior written notification to the appropriate registrar for the district in which the marriage is to take place. The courts may exempt a couple from either of these requirements, but a written exemption order must be obtained *before* the marriage takes place.

Until 1972, the minimum age for marriage in the Republic was based on Canon Law (the internal law of the Catholic Church) and was 14 years for boys and 12 years for girls. In 1972, the government passed the Marriages Act, which raised the minimum marriage age to 16 for boys and girls alike. Anyone aged between 16 and 21 had to have their parents' written consent to marry. Couples could apply to the courts for an exemption, but one third of all applications were refused. The 1995 Family Law Act raised the minimum age to 18.

Under that Act, any marriage – civil or religious – that does not comply with the new rules cannot be registered as a valid civil marriage. Anyone knowingly performing a marriage ceremony for a person under 18 would be guilty of a criminal offence and liable to a fine of €635 on conviction. The law applies to all marriages in the Republic of Ireland. The minimum age requirement also applies to marriages in any other country if either of the spouses is normally resident in Ireland.

That regulation creates anomalies, which will almost certainly lead to problems in the future. A 17-year-old resident of the Republic who lives in a cross-border parish and marries in Northern Ireland will be validly married in the North (where the minimum age for marriage is 17), but not in the Republic.

Also, if a person aged over 18 who is ordinarily resident in Ireland marries a person aged under 18 anywhere elsewhere in the world (for example, a 17-year-old in the UK), that marriage will not be recognised in Ireland.

If a parish straddles the border with Northern Ireland, for example, a priest who marries a 17-year-old parishioner in her own parish church would – depending on which side of the border she lived – either be contracting a valid and lawful marriage in the United Kingdom or committing a criminal offence in the Republic!

If either party to the marriage is under 18 and a court exemption has not been obtained, the registrar or person solemnising the marriage cannot go ahead with the ceremony. Anyone convicted of knowingly breaching the minimum age provisions is liable to a fine.

Evidence of age must be provided, if requested by a

registrar or anyone to whom application is made for a licence, certificate or the publication of banns, or the person who is to solemnise the marriage. If such evidence is not produced on request, the official may not go ahead with the marriage.

The 1995 Act allows the Circuit Family Court or the High Court to grant an exemption from the age limits or the notification requirements if both applicants show that the exemption is justified by serious reasons and is in the couple's best interests. It is an informal procedure and couples may apply in person without using a solicitor. There is no charge for such an application.

If a couple marry in church without abiding by the requirements of the act, they must subsequently marry in a civil ceremony, or they will remain unmarried as far as the state is concerned. That means that neither "spouse" can make use of marital legislation which applies only to married couples. Their children will be "non-marital" children and they will be unable to divorce because, as far as the civil courts are concerned, they were not married in the first place!

The 1995 Act allows either spouse to ask the court to rule that such a marriage is null and void – although it may not be necessary to make such an application if the facts are beyond dispute. The 1995 Regulations are *in addition* to previous regulations. Anyone who ignores these regulations may find that their marriage is not valid.

The three months' notification of a marriage may be given in either of two ways:

1. both parties may write – jointly or separately – to the appropriate (Catholic or civil) registrar of the district in which they are to marry, giving the names and addresses of both parties, the name of the church or place where the ceremony will take place, the proposed date of the marriage and the dates of birth of the couple (or confirmation that they are both over 18), or

2. a pre-printed form may be filled in and returned to the

local registrar (although, if only one form is sent in, both
parties must sign it.)

If the couple write jointly to the registrar, they must both
sign the letter. If they write separately, the required three
months runs from the receipt of the second letter. The notice
required is a *full* three months. (Limitation periods are
calculated differently under English and Irish law. In *McCann
v. An Bord Pleanála* (1997), the High Court said that, under
section 11 of the 1937 Interpretation Act, where a period of
time is reckonable from a certain day, that day is *included* in
the limitation period unless a contrary intention appears. So,
for example, a person giving notice on April 1 would be able
to marry on June 30.)

It is not necessary for anyone giving written notification
to provide the registrar with any documents about their age
(such as birth certificates) at the notification stage. If required,
the registrar will subsequently specifically request the
documents. There is no need to obtain parental consent for a
marriage if the parties are both over 18. If they are under 18,
it is up to the court to decide whether they should marry. If
either of the couple was previously married, the registrar
should be told at the time of notification.

Only original documents with original signatures may be
accepted as notification of intention to marry. The registrar
will issue an official receipt confirming the date of the
application, which must be produced on request to the person
solemnising the marriage.

The formalities relate to the two elements of marriage:
civil and religious. The appropriate registrar for the district
is determined by the form of the marriage. For the purposes
of the civil registration of a marriage, Catholics are treated
differently from non-Catholics and their marriages are
registered under a different Act.

Catholics who intend to have a Catholic Church marriage
must give notice of their intended marriage to the local

Registrar of Births, Deaths and (Catholic) Marriages. (Applications by divorced Catholics go the Registrar General.) Non-Catholics and anyone planning only a civil ceremony must give notice to the Registrar of Civil Marriages in their local district. Districts are usually – but not always – divided by county.

All marriages must take place in a registered, certified or licensed building if they are to be legal and civilly registered. Churches of the Church of Ireland are licensed for marriage by the Bishops of the Church with the approval – in the Republic – of the Minister for Health. Presbyterian churches are certified by the Church ministers and registered by the Registrar General. Anyone who wishes to be married in, for example, a hotel, should have a civil ceremony in an approved building first and a blessing in the hotel afterwards. If the marriage is in, for example, a Baptist chapel, at least one of the parties must be a Baptist.

The denominations whose premises are registered for marriages include the Catholic Church, Church of Ireland, Presbyterians, Methodists, Baptists, Greek Orthodox, Jews, Congregationalists, Quakers, Lutherans, Christian Brethren, Jehovah's Witnesses and Mormons (Latter Day Saints). Mosques are not registered for marriages because of the conflict between Shari'a (Islamic law) and Irish law on the issue of polygamy.

In the Supreme Court case of *Conlon v. Mohamed* (1988), Conlon was seeking possession of a house, which belonged to her partner, Mohamed. He claimed that he had validly married her, so the house was the marital home and he was entitled to remain in it. Mohamed was a citizen of South Africa and domiciled there. Conlon was a citizen of Ireland with a domicile in Ireland. In 1983, an Islamic marriage ceremony took place in a South African mosque. Conlon did not attend, but a male friend of Mohamed represented her. Later, the couple exchanged rings and vows at a separate ceremony. Mohamed said the exchange of rings and vows showed that the couple intended the mosque marriage to be monogamous. The couple planned to marry in a register office on their return to Dublin but never did so.

South African law did not recognise an Islamic marriage in a mosque or a marriage by proxy, and the marriage was also banned under South Africa's apartheid laws. The Supreme Court ruled that the couple had never been married, so the house was not a family home.

Marriage regulations are broken down into six areas:

(1) Catholics,

(2) Church of Ireland,

(3) Presbyterian,

(4) other Christians,

(5) Quakers and Jews and

(6) civil marriages.

The regulations are summarised as follows:

Catholic

Episcopal dispensation: Church rules apply. These now require three months' notice.

Publication of banns and special licence: do not apply.

Ordinary licence: seven days' notice. One party must be a Catholic. The licence is granted by the Bishop's nominee. A copy must be sent to the priest in the parish where the couple attend church.

Registrar's certificate: in a mixed marriage, where one party is non-Catholic. The registrar must be notified in the local district, giving full particulars of name, age, status and place of worship. He enters them in the marriage notice book and sends copies to the churches they attend and to the church where they will marry. A certificate will be issued 21 days later and the couple take it to the priest marrying them.

Solemnisation: marriage must be in public, in a Catholic church, in the presence of two witnesses. In *People v. Ballins* (1964), the judge said: "The decree of the Council of Trent has been promulgated in Ireland. It is applicable to and controls Roman Catholic marriages and makes the presence of two witnesses necessary. A ceremony not in accordance with its requirements as to the presence of a priest and two witnesses is null and void." It is the husband's duty to register the marriage.

Church of Ireland

Episcopal dispensation and registrar's licence: do not apply.

Publication of banns: regulated by the canons of the Church of Ireland and the rubrics of the prayer book. Both parties must be Protestant Episcopalians.

Ordinary licence: may be issued by the Bishop's nominees, appointed in specific districts. The licence authorises marriage in any church licensed for marriage in the licenser's district. At least one party must be a Protestant Episcopalian. One party must be resident in the district of the church where the marriage is to take place for seven days before the granting of the licence. The person to whom the licence is granted must have been living in the parish of the church where the wedding is to take place for at least 14 days. Before the licence is granted, one of the parties must appear before the licenser and swear an oath or declaration that there are no lawful impediments to the marriage. The licenser must enter a copy of the notice in the marriage notice book, open to the public at all reasonable times. It is the cleric's duty to register the marriage.

Special licence: issued by any Church of Ireland Bishop. One party must be a Protestant Episcopalian. The parties must return a certificate, signed by the couple, two witnesses and the clergyman, to the district registrar. The husband must register the marriage within three days.

Registrar's certificate: occasionally used.

Solemnisation: must be done publicly, in the presence of a cleric and two witnesses.

Presbyterians

Episcopal dispensation, registrar's certificate and registrar's licence: do not apply.

Publication of banns: no longer used in practice, though both parties would have to be Presbyterians.

Ordinary licence: one or both parties must be members of the Presbyterian Church in Ireland. Special ministers are appointed by the Presbyterian Church to grant the licence. The licence takes seven days to issue and the parties must obtain a certificate from their own minister stating that a notice of the marriage was entered in his congregation book. One of the parties must have been resident in the presbytery district for 15 days. An affirmation must be given that there are no impediments. The minister must enter the particulars in a notice book open at all reasonable times. Anyone may enter a caveat to the issue of the licence. If there is any dispute about the caveat, it may be referred to the Presbytery of the Church. If the marriage does not take place within one month of the date of the licence (or three months of the entry in the marriage notice book), the notice and licence are both void.

Special licence: granted by the Moderator of the General Assembly. One party must be a member of the Presbyterian Church in Ireland. A solemn declaration must be completed before a Justice of the Peace or a Peace Commissioner. A certificate of marriage by special licence must be sent to the Registrar General within three days of the marriage, completed and signed by the parties, two witnesses and the officiating minister.

Solemnisation: must be in public, in the presence of a minister and two or more witnesses. The marriage must be registered and entered in duplicate in the marriage registration book supplied by the Registrar General. The husband must register the marriage.

Other Christians

Episcopal dispensation, publication of banns and ordinary licence: do not apply.

Special licence: various officials (such as the Secretary of the Methodist Conference, the Chairman of the Congregational Union and the Moderator of the Reformed Presbyterian Church) can issue special licences.

Registrar's certificate: Same as for Catholics. The parties must give notice with all relevant details. The registrar files the notice, sends a copy to the place of worship and enters it in the marriage notice book open to the public at all reasonable times. The certificate is issued in 21 days.

Registrar's licence: notice must be given to the registrar, declaring in writing that there are no impediments to the marriage. Requirements concerning age and residency must be complied with. The registrar must file the notice, enter it in the marriage notice book, and notify the church attended and the church in which the couple intend to be married. The licence is issued in seven days and must be given to the cleric celebrating the marriage.

Solemnisation: in a registered building in the presence of a minister of religion of the creed of one or both parties and in the presence of two or more witnesses. The cleric must register the marriage in duplicate.

Quakers and Jews

Episcopal dispensation, publication of banns, registrar's licence and ordinary licence: do not apply.

Special licence: both parties must be Jews or Quakers. The licence is issued by the Chief Rabbi, or the Clerk to the yearly meeting.

Registrar's certificate: same as for "other Christians." The certificate is taken to the synagogue or meeting house. One party must be a non-Jew or non-Quaker.

Solemnisation: according to the beliefs of the parties, in public and in the presence of two or more witnesses. The person performing the ceremony has a duty to register the marriage.

Civil ceremony

Episcopal dispensation, publication of banns, ordinary licence and special licence: do not apply.

Registrar's certificate: both parties must establish seven full days' residence in their respective districts (in Ireland or the UK) and must be married in either of those districts. They must then serve notice on their respective District Registrars by personal attendance at the office. The ceremony may take place on the 22nd day after entry of the notice of marriage.

Registrar's licence: if both parties are resident in a district, they may marry eight days after serving notice. If they are not both resident in a district, one party must establish 15 full days' residence in the district and then serve notice on the Registrar. The other party can serve notice the same day if resident in the same district for seven full days (or by serving notice on their local registrar, if resident anywhere in Ireland). The marriage may take place on the eighth day after entry of notice by the Registrar.

(Notice and notification are two separate statutory requirements that must be fulfilled before the marriage can take place. "*Notice*" means the formal requirement of attending at the office of the registrar for him to complete a notice of marriage form and declaration of freedom to marry. Residency requirements must first be complied with. "*Notification*," which relates to the written three months' notice required under the 1995 Act, has no connection with residency.)

Normally, the marriage must take place in a register office, but if one of the parties is ill, the Registrar General may grant a special licence for the marriage to take place elsewhere.

Where either party to a civil marriage has been divorced, a certified copy of the decree absolute is required at the time of serving notice, together with the birth certificates of both parties to the divorce if born outside the state. If the decree is in a foreign language, a certified translation must be provided. The divorced party will also have to complete two questionnaires, one concerning each of the divorced spouses. The documents are subject to a check by the Registrar General, which can take five weeks or more.

The Domicile and Recognition of Foreign Divorces Act

1986 allows the recognition of UK divorces where *either* spouse was domiciled in the UK. Where *neither* spouse was domiciled in Ireland, a foreign divorce will be recognised here if it is recognised in the country where either spouse was domiciled.

In the case of *Paul Lambert v. The Registrar General of Marriages* (1995), Mr Lambert was domiciled in Ireland with his wife and children. In 1984, she left him and went to live in England with the children. Two years later she divorced him in England. Mr Lambert wanted to marry someone else in Ireland, but the Registrar General refused to issue a certificate because he said he wasn't satisfied that the former Mrs Lambert was domiciled in England at the time of the divorce. Mrs Lambert swore a declaration to say that she had intended to live permanently in England.

In the High Court, the judge said the registrar *was* entitled to investigate the circumstances of the divorce, but the question of the former wife's domicile was partly a matter of law – which was a matter for the courts, not the registrar. The judge said the court was entitled to act on Mrs Lambert's uncontradicted declaration, and he ruled that Mr Lambert was free to remarry.

A divorce or nullity decree granted in any EU country except Denmark after March 1, 2001 is automatically recognised in Ireland. Article 14.2 of EC Regulation 1347/2000 says that:

> "no special procedure is required to update the civil records of a member state on the basis of a final judgment relating to divorce, legal separation or marriage annulment given in another member state (after March 1 2001)."

Where either party is widowed, a certified copy of the death certificate and the original marriage certificate must be produced at the time of serving notice.

Where either party has been granted a civil nullity decree, a certified copy of the decree must be produced when serving notice, together with a statement from the Supreme Court (or appropriate court in any other EU country) that no appeal has been lodged against the decree.

If a couple aged 18 or over wish to marry outside Ireland (for example in Rome), they must ensure that they comply with the legal requirements of marriage in that country. The embassy for that country should be able to give details and explain how to obtain a marriage certificate. Such marriages are not normally registered in Ireland.

A certificate of freedom to marry (also known as a *certificat de coûtume* or certificate of *nulla osta*) may be required in some countries. The certificate, which states that a person is not already married, may be obtained from the consular section of the Department of Foreign Affairs. Irish citizens living abroad may obtain the certificate from their nearest Irish embassy.

If you are concerned about whether your own marriage conformed to the necessary formalities, you should contact a family law solicitor.

Chapter Six

Civil Nullity

Before divorce became available, nullity was one of the few ways of ending a "marriage." But with the passing of the Divorce Act, nullity has become a less important concept in the family law courts. The number of nullity decrees had been rising steadily before divorce was introduced. In 1981, eight nullity decrees were granted. By 1990, that figure had risen to 30 and by 1997 to 53. Following the introduction of divorce, the number of nullity applications almost halved, from 86 (in 1995/96) to 48 the following year.

But even today, nullity may be a preferable option for some people. A person who has recently married, for example, and believes he or she may have been pressurised into marriage or incapable of giving proper consent, may wish to obtain a civil nullity decree, rather than wait four years for a divorce.

Equally, for a spouse who wishes to avoid the financial implications of a divorce, a nullity – if available – may be a much more attractive option. The couple would both be treated as single persons and the issue of joint marital property or the Family Home Protection Act would not arise.

It is crucial, therefore, to receive proper advice from an experienced family law solicitor before taking any action that could prejudice an application for a nullity decree by approbation of the marriage (such as the use of family law legislation).

Marriage was defined by Lord Penzance, in *Hyde v. Hyde and Woodmansee* (1866), as "the voluntary union for life of one man and one woman to the exclusion of all others".

If, for example, the union is not voluntary, or the parties are not male and female, the relationship may never have been a marriage. The courts have jurisdiction to rule whether or not a civil marriage is valid or whether it is null and void.

The jurisdiction of the Irish courts to deal with matrimonial matters dates back more than 125 years. Until the late nineteenth century, the established Church – the Church of Ireland – had exclusive jurisdiction to deal with matrimonial causes. But, with the disestablishment of the Church, the civil courts took over.

The 1870 Matrimonial Causes and Marriage Law Act said the principles and rules of civil nullity should approximate to Church rules. That is still the case today, and the grounds on which a civil court will grant a decree of nullity are much the same as the grounds for a Church nullity. Judge Henchy, in *N. (orse K.) v. K.* (1986), said the 1870 Act did not fossilise the law, but the civil doctrine of nullity nevertheless remained largely unchanged until quite recently.

When the court grants a decree of nullity, it is ruling that the marriage never existed – with all the implications that may have for the legal rights of the couple.

A nullity decree has little or nothing to do with the circumstances at the time of the application, but everything to do with the situation at the time of the "marriage".

For example, in *A.C. (orse J.) v. P.J.* (1995), a mother of five children was granted a decree of nullity. The woman had become pregnant when she was 21. She was a country girl from a strict religious background and was so afraid to tell her family about the pregnancy that she was admitted to a psychiatric hospital suffering from acute anxiety. She was discharged from hospital the day before the wedding. The couple eventually had five children. The judge in the High Court said the woman's consent to the marriage was not a full and free exercise of her independent will, and he granted her a decree of nullity.

Although a couple is not legally required to obtain a decree of nullity where a marriage is void, it would be sensible for them to obtain the High Court's recognition of the *status quo*, in case of legal difficulties later when attempting to remarry or if the other party claims that the marriage is valid. The court has power to declare a marriage valid or invalid. Anybody with an interest in the matter – not just the couple themselves – may apply for a nullity decree in the case of a void marriage.

To contract a valid marriage in this State, the parties must:

(1) have the capacity to marry each other,

(2) freely consent to the marriage and

(3) observe the formalities required by Irish law.

The six grounds which will render a marriage *void* are:

- an existing previous marriage (including remarriage after a divorce not recognised in Ireland, or after a Church nullity without a civil decree),

- where either party was under 18 at the time of the marriage without a prior court exemption,

- non-observance of formalities, such as the three months' notice (although minor flaws are not necessarily fatal),

- absence of consent (including duress, undue influence, fraud and mental illness)

- where parties are within the forbidden degrees of blood relationship or are the same sex.

The law in this area is complex and can best be understood by considering the application of the principles in real cases.

For a marriage to be valid, any consent must be a "fully free exercise of the independent will of the parties". In *N. (orse K.) v. K.* (1985), the petitioner, who was a 19-year-old virgin, became pregnant after a short and casual relationship.

She was an unassertive and obedient girl, and her parents thought she should marry the baby's father. She agreed to marry but later sought a decree of nullity on the grounds of duress.

The High Court refused a decree because it said the parties had intended to marry anyway, but the Supreme Court allowed an appeal. It said duress was not restricted to threats of physical harm or other harmful consequences. If the decision to marry was "caused by external pressure or influence, whether falsely or honestly applied, to such an extent as to lose the character of a fully free act of that person's will, no valid marriage had occurred."

In *D.B. (orse O'R.) v. N. O'R.* (1988), the judge said a marriage was invalid if induced by "fear of threats, intimidation, duress or undue influence". Fraud may also negative consent where it relates to a fundamental feature of the marriage (*S. v. S.*)1976))

In *Griffith v. Griffith* (1944), a 19-year-old was told he'd be sent to jail if he didn't marry a pregnant girl. He realised later he couldn't have been the child's father. He was granted an annulment, as his consent was obtained by fear and fraud.

In *B. v. D.* (1973), the judge said the "forceful arrogance" of the husband amounted to duress and the marriage was therefore invalid. In *S. v. O'S.* (1978), the High Court said there was no freedom of will when one party was in the "emotional bondage" of the other. In *C. O'K. (orse C.P.) v. W.P.* (1984), the judge said attempts by a violent and domineering 18-year-old youth to obtain the consent of a quiet 16-year-old girl amounted to duress and undue influence.

In *P.W. v A. O'C. (orse W.)* (1991), the petitioner husband had married in a Catholic Church in London in 1956 after his fiancée threatened to gas herself or throw herself under a train if he did not marry her immediately. In 1979, the husband obtained a Catholic Church nullity and, in 1981, he went through a ceremony of marriage with another woman. He was indicted for bigamy but subsequently acquitted. He was granted a decree of nullity on the grounds of duress.

The judge in *M.K. (orse M. McC.) v. F. McC.* (1982) said the will of a reluctant 19-year-old bride and a resentful 21-year-old husband was overborne by their parents. But in *E.P. v. M.C.* (1985), the judge refused a decree where a pregnant girl had threatened abortion unless her boyfriend married her.

Pre-existing pregnancy is not, in itself, sufficient to invalidate a person's free consent. In *A.C.L. v. R.L.* (1982), the judge said a couple aged 28 and 32 with a baby had intended to marry at some stage and he refused a decree. And in *K.W. v. M.W.* (1994), where the petitioner claimed he was pressured into marrying his 17-year-old pregnant girlfriend, the judge said he was satisfied that the couple had contemplated marriage at some stage, and refused a decree.

Pre-existing mental illness might be grounds for dissolving a marriage. In *R.S.J. v. J.S.J.* (1982), where the husband petitioned after an eight-month marriage because of his schizophrenia, the judge said the husband had understood the nature, purpose and consequences of marriage. If it were voidable, it would only be on the wife's application. But if, through illness at the date of marriage, a petitioner lacked the capacity to form a caring and considerate relationship, the judge might consider it grounds for nullity.

Indeed, in *D. v. C.* (1984), the judge said a husband's manic depression before, during and after marriage severely impaired his capacity to form and sustain a normal marriage. The judge said:

> "It should be recognised that there have been important scientific advances in the field of psychiatric medicine since 1870 and that it is now possible to identify psychiatric illness, such as for example manic depressive illness, which in many cases may be so severe as to make it impossible for one of the partners to the marriage to enter into and sustain the relationship which should exist between married couples if a lifelong union

is to be possible."

And in *D.C. v. D.W.* (1986), the judge granted a decree to a schizophrenic wife on her own petition.

In *B.D. v. M.C. (orse M.D.)* (1987), the judge accepted a wife's emotional immaturity as grounds for nullity. In *W. v. P.* (1984), the judge allowed the petition of the wife of a suicidal farmer who had an emotional age of five.

The mental illness must have existed at the time of the marriage. In *S.C. v. P.D. (orse C.)* (1996), SC was seeking a decree of nullity after 22 years of marriage and three children. A month before the first baby was born, the wife had an episode of hypermania. She showed the same symptoms during her second and third pregnancy, suffering from acute hypermania, grandiose delusions and bizarre ideas.

Mr Justice Brian McCracken said that the wife's manic depression did not affect her ability to have marital relations unless triggered by some event. He said a person could not be granted a nullity if suffering from a latent illness which did not affect the ability to enter into marriage, but which might subsequently affect the ability to sustain the marriage.

More rarely, a person may seek a decree of nullity because the parties were not respectively male and female. In the case of *Corbett v. Corbett (orse Ashley)* (1971), a 40-year-old transvestite left his wife and family and married 25-year-old transsexual George Jamieson, who'd had a sex-change operation in Casablanca in 1960. After the operation, Mr Jamieson lived as a woman and called himself April Ashley. He was courted by Arthur Corbett (Lord Rowallan) and they married in Gibraltar in 1963.

They split up after 14 days and Lord Rowallan petitioned for a declaration of nullity on the basis either that April was a castrated man or because of April's inability or refusal to consummate the marriage. Nine doctors gave evidence in what the judge called a "pathetic but almost incredible story". The court ruled that the respondent was at all times a male, so the marriage was void.

In another English case, *S.-T. v. J.* (1998), the defendant had been born a female but underwent a partial sex change some time before the marriage. For 17 years, the wife remained unaware of her "husband's" true gender until the production of the birth certificate at a divorce hearing. As a result, the wife applied for and was granted a decree of nullity.

More commonly, a marriage is not void *ab initio* (from the beginning), but is "voidable," which means that it remains valid until a competent tribunal declares otherwise.

The two grounds for *voidable* marriage are:

• physical impotence, and

• inability to enter into and sustain a normal marital relationship.

A marriage is "voidable" where, for example, one of the partners was psychologically incapable at the time of the marriage of forming "a caring or considerate relationship". Such a marriage would be valid until a competent authority declared otherwise.

In *McK. v. McK.* (1936), a wife said she had an "invincible repugnance" to her husband, and the judge said he should use a "little bit of gentle violence" on her! In *W. v. W.* (1980) the wife was granted a decree based on her own – rather than her husband's – psychological incapacity. The High Court said the husband had repudiated the marriage by seeking a Church nullity and it granted a decree of civil nullity.

In *H.F. (orse H.C.) v. J.C.* (1990), the judge refused a nullity to a wife on grounds of her husband's prior homosexuality, as it would add new grounds under the 1870 Act. On appeal, the Chief Justice said incapacity by virtue of prior homosexuality – where the petitioner was unaware of this – was grounds for nullity. (Incapacity is a ground for nullity, comparable to impotence.)

In *M.J. v. C.J.* (1991), a wife was granted a decree of

nullity because her husband admitted three days after the wedding that he had been involved with a mother-of-two until just before the marriage. He had previously denied the relationship.

On the other hand, in 1999, the High Court refused a decree of nullity to a man whose wife had an affair with her employer shortly after the marriage. The man – known by the initials P.F. – claimed that, if he had known she was having an affair, he would not have married her. He said his consent to the marriage was not "full, free and informed."

Mr Justice O'Higgins concluded that the allegations were true, but said the "nondisclosure of inappropriate behaviour" before or during courtship was not a ground for nullity. "It is not incumbent on the parties to give a history of their good or bad behaviour prior to getting married in order to contract a valid marriage," he said. "In this case, the parties had a courtship which lasted several years. They knew prior to getting married the nature of the contract they were undertaking." The Supreme Court agreed and dismissed his appeal.

Even flagrant sexual infidelity by one spouse is seldom sufficient for a nullity decree. In *P.C. v. C.M. (orse C.)* (1996), P.C. was seeking a decree of nullity after six years of marriage. His wife, C.M., claimed the marriage was valid but had irretrievably broken down. When the couple met, she already had a baby. P.C. and C.M. saw each other regularly, but eventually broke up and C.M. continued her sexual relationship with the child's father.

Later P.C. bought a house, took C.M. to see it and asked whether it would be "all right", which she took as a proposal of marriage. They married in 1989, but a year later, she said she wanted to end the marriage. She left home for four days and had sex with the boy's father again. When she returned, the couple tried to sort out their difficulties and saw a counsellor, but in 1993, the counsellor also started a sexual relationship with C.M. In 1994, the husband petitioned for nullity. A consultant psychiatrist said the wife had an immature personality disorder at the time of the marriage.

Mrs Justice Laffoy said the wife had been "flagrantly unfaithful" to her husband, but was able to understand the nature, purpose and consequence of the marriage contract and had entered into the marriage with good intent. She refused a decree of nullity.

Emotional or psychological immaturity at the time of the marriage may be grounds for a nullity decree. In *P.C. v. V.C.* (1989), the judge said a marriage was doomed from the outset by reasons of the couple's immaturity. He said there was lack of emotional capacity and psychological weakness on both sides. Delay was not evidence of approval of the marriage, but of confusion. Temperamental incapacity alone was insufficient for a decree, but in this case there was also want of capacity, so the judge declared the marriage null and void.

In *N. (orse K.) v. K.* (1985), the Supreme Court had ruled that for, a marriage to be valid, the consent of each spouse – in addition to being freely given – must be informed.

In the case of *M. O'M. (otherwise O'C.) v. B. O'C.* (1996), a wife appealed against the High Court's refusal to grant her a decree of nullity. Before the marriage, her husband had been a priest. After ordination in 1972, he worked for four years as a curate but found the life lonely and difficult and attended a psychiatrist from 1976 to 1982, when he was laicised. He married his wife in 1985 when he was 37 and she was 32. They had two children and separated in 1989 (though they were still living in the same house when the wife brought her petition in 1994).

The wife, who did not know of her husband's psychiatric treatment, told the High Court she was "completely stunned" when she learned that her husband had been attending a psychiatrist for seven years. "I certainly would not have married him because, those kind of psychiatric illnesses, you get remission but you never get a cure," she said.

But the judge said both parties were capable of entering

into, maintaining and sustaining a proper marriage relationship. He also found that the wife gave a full, free and informed consent to the marriage. He refused a decree and the wife appealed. In the Supreme Court, Mr Justice Blayney said:

> "A person's mental health or mental stability is obviously a matter of great importance and anything which might throw doubt upon it calls for serious consideration.

> "The test is subjective. It is possible that another person would not have reacted in the same way, but this was the wife's evidence of how she would have reacted if she had known."

He allowed the appeal and declared the marriage null and void because the wife's consent was not informed.

If a nullity petition is brought in the Circuit Court and the result is appealed to the High Court that is normally the end of the matter. The Courts' (Supplemental Provisions) Act 1961 says that every Circuit Court order in civil matters can be appealed to the High Court, whose decision will be final.

The courts have constantly stressed the need for finality in all proceedings. As Lord Simon said in the *Ampthill Peerage* case (1977) in England: "Since judges and juries are fallible human beings, we have provided appellate courts which do their own fallible best to correct error. But in the end you must accept what has been decided. Enough is enough."

In the case of *P. v. P.* (2001), the appellant husband argued that he had been denied a fair hearing in the High Court, so should be allowed a further appeal. His wife had initiated Circuit Court proceedings relating to the custody of the children, access, right of residence in the family home and maintenance. The Circuit Court heard the case in March 1999 and the husband appealed the decision to the High Court.

The appeal came before the High Court a year later. After hearing opening submissions from counsel – but before hearing any evidence – the judge said: "Without making any final conclusions because I have not heard the evidence, but from what little I have heard about this case, it seems to me that this is the classic situation where the family budget is too small."

The husband said that, because of the judge's bias, he did not wish to proceed with his appeal. His counsel argued that the Supreme Court could set aside a final High Court order where there had been a fundamental breach of the constitutional right to a fair and proper hearing.

But Mr Justice Murray said the husband should first have brought a High Court application to have the judge's order set aside. He dismissed the appeal on the grounds that the Supreme Court had no jurisdiction to hear it.

Civil nullity is rarely a straightforward matter and it may be difficult to assess whether a case will succeed or fail because of the wide disparity in the case law. In the 1999 *P.F.* case, a Supreme Court judge called on the government to clarify the law on nullity.

Mrs Justice Catherine McGuinness said that, in the days when divorce was unavailable in Ireland, there might have been some advantage in allowing the courts to develop the law of nullity. Now that judicial separation and divorce were both available, the Oireachtas should provide a clear statutory code setting out the grounds for nullity and its consequences for the couple and any children.

But, despite the uncertainty in the law, a decree of nullity may still have distinct advantages (and corresponding disadvantages) when compared to a decree of divorce. Anyone considering annulment would be well advised to consult a solicitor who is knowledgeable in this complicated area of the law.

Chapter Seven

Judicial Separation

If a marriage is found to be valid, there can be no decree of nullity. If the partners in such a marriage wish to go their own ways, they have two choices: separation or divorce. Before the Reformation, marriage was regarded by the law as a sacrament and the duty of cohabitation – the main duty arising from the marriage contract – was enforced by the Church with spiritual punishments *pro salute animae* (for the health of the soul). Voluntary separations were forbidden by law, and contracts for voluntary separations were invalid. But under Henry VIII, Church law was subordinated to the common law and voluntary separations became permissible.

Separation nowadays may be by agreement or by order of the court (a decree of judicial separation). The only effect of a judicial separation order is to give the couple the right to live apart, and to deal with all the incidental matters which arise when a marriage breaks down, such as children, property adjustment, the family home, maintenance payments and succession rights.

Under the 1870 Matrimonial Causes Act, the only grounds on which a divorce could be granted were adultery, cruelty and unnatural practices. The ancillary relief was limited to orders for alimony and custody. The decree deprived the guilty spouse of the right to a share in the estate of the other spouse, either as a legal right or on intestacy.

The procedure for a divorce *a mensa et thoro* ("from table and bed") did not alter in any way the status of the husband and wife. The only effect of the order – apart from the ancillary reliefs – was to relieve the petitioning spouse from the duty to cohabit with the other. Although called divorce, it was effectively a decree of judicial separation and did not allow remarriage. (As well as the power to allow a couple to live separately, the courts could also theoretically require a couple to live together as man and wife!)

In the overwhelming majority of cases, the parties were already living apart, so the decree was frequently of little significance. These proceedings were normally brought solely to obtain ancillary relief or to remove the succession rights of the spouse described as the "guilty party".

In 1981, the courts' jurisdiction to oblige couples to live together, by ordering the restitution of conjugal rights, was removed by the Family Law Act. Eight years later, the Judicial Separation and Family Law Reform Act removed the courts' jurisdiction to grant a divorce *a mensa et thoro*. Instead, the High Court and Circuit Court were given power to grant decrees of judicial separation.

The 1989 Act significantly extended the grounds on which such a decree could be granted. It also widened the range of ancillary reliefs to include periodical payments and lump sum orders, property adjustment orders, orders extinguishing succession rights and miscellaneous ancillary orders.

In 1990, there were 636 applications for judicial separation. Within four years, the number of applications had risen more than four-fold to 2,847. The numbers began to fall after the introduction of divorce, with only 1,208 applications in 1997, but that decline turned out to be only temporary. Ever since, the numbers have risen steadily, with a total of 1,845 judicial separation applications to the Circuit Court in 2001 – more than four out of five of those being made by women.

Although the High Court can also grant a judicial separation, more than 97% of judicial separations are granted by the Circuit Family Court.

The constitutional validity of the 1989 Judicial Separation and Family Law Reform Act was challenged in the case of

T.F. v. Ireland and M.F. (1995). MF had obtained a Circuit Court decree of judicial separation from her husband, T.F., on the grounds that a normal marital relationship had not existed for at least a year. She also obtained a permanent barring order against her husband and was awarded custody of the children.

The husband said the Act's presumption that a marriage had broken down where no normal marital relationship had existed for one year didn't allow enough time for a reconciliation and set too low a threshold for an order which would impair his marital rights under the Constitution. He also claimed that sections of the Act which granted his wife the right to live in the family home for life and which provided a dependent spouse with accommodation after a judicial separation were an attack on his Constitutional property rights.

The High Court refused to hear evidence from theologians in relation to natural moral law or the essential features of a Christian marriage, and the judge dismissed the husband's claim. He said that, while the concept of marriage referred to in Article 41.3.1° might be derived from the Christian concept of marriage, it was up to the courts – not the Churches – to interpret those rights.

He said all the basic rights in a marriage, such as the right to have children, to live together, to give and receive moral and financial support and to make decisions relating to family property were protected by Article 40.3 of the Constitution. But he said those rights were not unqualified and their exercise could be regulated by the Oireachtas in the interests of the common good.

Any interpretation of the Constitution should take account of changing ideas and values. Nowadays, he said, a married woman no longer had to live in "an unacceptable state of bondage."

The judge said it appeared that the one-year rule was justified, particularly as the separation proceedings could be adjourned by consent. There were serious difficulties in trying to provide an objective measurement of success or failure in reconciliation therapy. It depended on whether the husband and wife were sincerely trying to be reconciled or just attending as a matter of form.

The breakdown of a marriage meant there was no physical capacity to consummate the marriage and no emotional and psychological relationship between the spouses. If one party was implacably opposed to the continuation of the marriage, the fundamental relationship would be destroyed.

The judge said a decree of judicial separation merely meant that the husband and wife no longer had to live together. It did not affect the bond of marriage or prevent the couple getting back together again. The grant of a decree based on the absence of a normal marital relationship was little more than a recognition of an existing, and usually tragic, state of affairs.

On the issue of the family home, the courts had long recognised that the home had a psychological value as a point of unity around which the children of a broken marriage might preserve or rebuild some of the relationships on which a family's development depended.

An order giving a spouse the sole right to live in the family home merely conferred a right of residence, not a right of ownership, and it could be balanced by a reduction in maintenance. The power to grant a right of residence to one spouse was not an unjust attack on the property rights of either party, but just one feature of the "difficult and unhappy task" of trying to balance the best interests of both spouses and their dependent children.

On appeal, the Supreme Court said it had to decide whether the balance of the legislation was so unreasonable and unfair as to be an attack on Constitutional rights.

The five judges said the Constitution protected the institution of marriage because of its contribution to the welfare of the nation and the State. The State's guarantee to protect the family was given to every married couple.

The concept and nature of marriage in the Constitution were derived from the Christian notion of partnership based on an irrevocable personal consent given by both spouses, which established a unique and very special lifelong relationship (as stated by Mr Justice Declan Costello in *Murray v. Ireland* (1985)). Marriage was also a civil contract that created reciprocating duties and rights between the couple and established a status, which affected both parties to the contract and the community as a whole.

One of those rights and duties was cohabitation, without which the "unique and very special lifelong relationship" could not be developed. But, in many cases, the common good required that the spouses should be separated, despite the nature of the indissoluble bond of marriage between them. If one spouse withdrew consent to cohabitation, it could not be enforced. Where such consent was withdrawn, an important ingredient of the normal marital relationship was removed, although the bond of marriage remained.

The party in breach of the marriage contract was entitled to seek a judicial separation, but, in view of the numerous other rights safeguarded by the Act, the entitlement to a decree in such circumstances was not a failure to protect the institution of marriage. The legislation made every effort to protect the family after a marriage broke down.

The judges said that the provision of grounds for judicial separation did not mean that the State had failed to "guard with special care the institution of marriage or protect it against attack." The court said that anyone who claimed that the one-year period in the Act was inadequate had to prove that was the case.

The right of one spouse to occupy the family home had to be seen in the context of that part of the Act which aimed to ensure that, as far as practicable, provision was made for the whole family, so the right of sole residence in the family home and the provision of proper accommodation for the dependent spouse and children were not an unjust attack on the property rights of the spouse who was excluded from the home. The Supreme Court dismissed the appeal.

The principal effect of a decree of judicial separation – to free the spouses from their duty to cohabit – is often the least of their worries. The problems that have led to the couple consulting lawyers may often have already resulted in a cessation – to a greater or lesser degree – of normal marital relations.

The decree does not *compel* the couple to separate, and a different order is required to exclude one of the spouses from the family home.

The advantage of a decree under the 1989 Act (and the 1995 Act) is that it gives the spouses access to a wide range of secondary remedies, including financial provisions, property adjustment and the occupation of the family home. (The 1995 Act changed much of the 1989 Act dealing with financial, property, custody and other orders. Under the 1995 Act, there is no limit to the number of occasions on which the court can grant a property adjustment order, except that it can't be granted after the death or remarriage of the respondent spouse.)

A court is barred from considering an application for a judicial separation if the couple had earlier been granted a decree of divorce *a mensa et thoro*.

In the case of *F. v. F.* (1995), a wife had sought a decree of divorce *a mensa et thoro* and a barring order against her husband in 1986. The proceedings were settled by agreement, on the basis that the husband would stay away from the family home and neither party would interfere with the other.

In 1992 the wife tried to bring proceedings for judicial separation against her husband and claimed a permanent barring order, a property adjustment order and the removal of her husband's rights to succeed to her estate.

The Supreme Court ruled that the earlier proceedings barred the wife from bringing a new action under the 1989

Act. The Chief Justice said the court would not support an action where a separation was sought merely as a way of obtaining other reliefs.

A couple may also not seek a judicial separation if they already have a separation agreement in force. In *P. O'D. v. A. O'D.* (1997), the couple had signed a separation deed in 1979. Later, the husband claimed a judicial separation but the wife said the court could not grant a judicial separation where the husband and the wife were no longer obliged to live together because of the separation agreement.

Her solicitor said it was not open to the husband to issue proceedings seeking a relief, which he did not need (i.e. a decree of judicial separation) just so that he could obtain a property order to which he would not otherwise be entitled.

Counsel for the husband said the 1989 Act did not prevent parties to separation agreements from applying for a judicial separation. He said the situation would be different if the husband and the wife had agreed not to take any further proceedings.

But the Supreme Court said the separation agreement was a comprehensive disposal of the issues that had arisen between the husband and the wife, and she was entitled to rely on the agreement as a bar to the judicial separation proceedings.

If a person consults a solicitor about the possibility of a judicial separation, the solicitor is required first to discuss the possibility of reconciliation and provide the applicant with a list of names and addresses of qualified marriage counsellors.

If there is no prospect of reconciliation, the solicitor must advise about mediation and provide a list of qualified mediators. If the couple finally decide to separate, the possibility of a separation agreement must also be discussed.

The solicitor must file a certificate to confirm that he has complied with the Act. If he fails to do so, the court may adjourn the proceedings until the certificate has been filed.

Judicial separation proceedings are heard in private and

are as informal as practicable, consistent with justice. (Judges and lawyers do not wear wigs or gowns in family law proceedings.) A judicial separation is only available to married couples and the 1989 Act allows a decree of judicial separation on six grounds:

- adultery,

- unreasonable behaviour,

- one year's continuous desertion,

- one year's separation (with consent),

- three years' separation (without consent), or

- no normal marital relationship for at least a year.

An application for judicial separation need not be restricted to a single ground. Frequently claims of unreasonable behaviour and the absence of a normal marital relationship are included in a single application.

The Act says that an applicant may not allege adultery as a basis for a decree of judicial separation if the couple have lived together for a year after the alleged adultery became known to the other spouse. Unreasonable behaviour may not be pleaded if the couple live together for more than six months after the last alleged incident of such behaviour.

One of the grounds for judicial separation is "that the respondent has behaved in such a way that the applicant cannot reasonably be expected to live with the respondent." Under the old ground of cruelty for a decree of divorce *a mensa et thoro*, an applicant had to prove conduct which made it unsafe for him or her to live with the other spouse (*Carpenter v. Carpenter* (1827), *McA. v. McA.* (1981)). That is no longer necessary, but the applicant now has to show that, as a result of the other spouse's behaviour, it is no longer reasonable to expect the couple to live together.

In the case of *Murphy v. Murphy* (1962), the President of

the High Court said the husband's conduct had resulted in a situation "where common life became impossible." The judge said that, while individual incidents were trivial in themselves, their cumulative effect could be serious. In the case of *B.L. v. M.L.* (1988), the husband's behaviour included violence, verbal abuse and false allegations about his wife.

A further ground for judicial separation is that the marriage has broken down to the extent that the court is satisfied that a normal marital relationship has not existed between the spouses for at least one year immediately before the date of the application.

In *K. v. K.* (1990), a decree was granted on this basis, but the Circuit Court didn't order the husband to leave the family home. The judge refused to grant the wife a barring order but gave her the sole right to occupy the family home for life because section 10(2)(a) of the 1995 Act says the court must take into consideration that "where a decree of judicial separation is granted, it is not possible for the spouses concerned to continue to reside together".

There is no need for proof of *irretrievable* breakdown. The court will require evidence that the couple's relationship is so different from a reasonably normal relationship that it may conclude the marriage has broken down. The situation must have continued for at least a year before the application. Fault, under this ground, is irrelevant and there is no requirement for proof of intolerable behaviour by the respondent.

The document, which is issued to begin judicial separation proceedings, is called an *application.* The person seeking the separation is the *applicant* and the other spouse is the *respondent.*

Once the judicial separation application has been issued, and before the court rules on the case, a spouse may seek preliminary orders to ensure proper financial provision for her and the children until the hearing of the action.

Before the full hearing of the judicial separation case, a

spouse may also seek orders including a *barring order* (preventing the other spouse entering the family home), a *custody* (or *access) order* in relation to any dependent children and orders for the protection of the family home, furniture and personal belongings.

The court will not grant a judicial separation unless it's satisfied that arrangements have been made for the welfare of any dependent children, including custody, access and matters relating to the children's "religious and moral, intellectual, physical and social welfare." Custody will generally be left to the parents to decide but, if they can't agree, the court will make a decision.

Once a decree has been granted, the court may make an order for periodical payments (or maintenance) in favour of the dependent spouse and children up to the age of 18 (or 23 if in full-time education), or mentally or physically disabled persons. Such provision must be "adequate and reasonable, having regard to all the circumstances".

For many years, the English courts operated what was known as "the one third rule", whereby the wife received about one third of the husband's income as maintenance plus about one third of the capital assets of the family. but, as Lord Denning said in *Wachtel v. Wachtel* (1973):

> "This proposal is not a rule. It is only a starting point. It will serve in cases where the marriage has lasted for many years and the wife has been in the home bringing up the children. It may not be applicable where the marriage has lasted only a short time, or where there are no children and she can go out to work."

The Supreme Court confirmed that the "one third rule" should only be used as a rough guide. In *T. v. T.* (2002), Mrs Justice Susan Denham said:

> "The concept of one third as a check on fairness may

well be useful in some cases, however it may have no application in many cases.

"It may not be applicable to a family with inadequate assets. It may not be relevant to a family of adequate means if, for example, such a sum could only be achieved by a sale of assets that would destroy a business, or the future income of a party or parties, or if it related to property brought solely by one party to the marriage, or any other relevant circumstance. It may not be applicable to a situation where a party has wealth from his or her own endeavours to which the other party has no claim except under section 20 (of the Family Law (Divorce) Act)."

The court is entitled to consider all the assets of a couple, including those obtained before marriage or by inheritance. In *M. v. M.* (2001), a wife sought a share in the £1.4 million proceeds of sale of a farm, which had been inherited by the husband and had been leased out during the marriage. The husband said the proceeds did not form part of the "matrimonial property" and he should keep the full amount.

But the judge held that there was no concept of "matrimonial property" in Irish law as there was in other legal systems. He said there was nothing in the legislation that limited the extent of the spouses' assets, which the court could consider when making orders.

The husband had been awarded custody of the children and would need to buy a suitable house. The judge said an equal division of the sale proceeds would be unfair, so he awarded the wife £350,000, to include the proceeds of the sale of the family home, of which she was half owner.

If one spouse tries to dispose of assets within three years of a judicial separation or divorce, the other spouse may challenge that disposition. Alternatively, a spouse may apply to the court to prevent such a disposition. There is a presumption that such dispositions are intended to deprive a spouse of relief.

Even the sale of shares may be affected. In *L. O'M. v. N. O'M. (orse N. McC.)* (2001), the High Court ruled that shares in a number of building companies which were developing and selling houses constituted personal property, and a spouse could be prevented from selling them.

Before making any order, the court must consider "the income, earning capacity, property and other financial resources which each of the spouses concerned has, or is likely to have in the foreseeable future." In almost all cases, the court accepts that the standard of living of both spouses will be reduced following a separation or divorce.

The maintenance order may be backdated to the date of issue of the judicial separation application. If the husband is employed and there have been problems with payment of maintenance, there could be an attachment of earnings order, whereby payments would be deducted at source by his employer.

The court will take into account both spouses' salaries and any child allowance or social welfare. It will also consider the length of the marriage, the spouses' ages and their future earning capacity. The maintenance order in respect of each child stops automatically when the child ceases to be dependent.

The court may also order a spouse to pay a lump sum for expenses and liabilities and may direct that periodical and lump sum payments be secured, possibly by the transfer of property to trustees. The court may also make property adjustment orders to achieve a fair distribution of property, including the family home. "Proper and secure accommodation" should, where practicable, be provided for a spouse who is wholly or mainly dependent on the other spouse, and for any dependent child.

Frequently, the court will grant the wife and children the right to occupy the family home, at least until the children have all ceased to be dependent. The husband's ability to provide a home for himself would be taken into account. Thereafter, the court could consider the contributions each of the spouses has made to the home and might well come to the conclusion, as the court did in *Wachtel v. Wachtel* (1973), that the family home should be regarded as the joint property of both.

The court may later vary the order relating to the occupation of the family home and make an order for its sale and division of the proceeds.

If a couple are subsequently reconciled, the court may rescind the separation decree by consent, if the judge is satisfied that a reconciliation has taken place and the couple wish to resume (or have already resumed) co-habitation as man and wife.

Chapter Eight

Divorce

Divorce was introduced to Ireland by the Family Law (Divorce) Act, which came into force on February 27, 1997. Once a divorce is granted, both parties are free to remarry. A court has no power to restrict the remarriage of a divorced person, no matter what the grounds for divorce.

Since the introduction of divorce, the number of applications has risen steadily. In the first full year, 2,725 people applied to the Circuit Court for a divorce. In 2001, almost 3,500 applications for divorce were received by Circuit Courts around the country. Only one was refused. More than 60 % of the applicants were women.

Just over 15,000 applications for divorce had been received by the courts up to the end of 2001 – though that seemed low compared with estimates at the time of the divorce referendum that there were 80,000 or so people in broken marriages.

A solicitor consulted by someone seeking a divorce must first discuss with the client the prospect of reconciliation, and provide a list of people qualified to help resolve the couple's problems. He must also discuss the possibility of mediation (to help the couple agree the terms of the separation or divorce) and give the client a list of qualified mediators. Thirdly, the solicitor must discuss the alternatives of judicial separation or a written separation agreement.

A register of professional organisations qualified to help couples in difficulty was to be compiled under the provisions of the 1996 Divorce Act. The cost of any mediation or counselling is at the court's discretion.

If divorce proceedings are issued, the other spouse must also be given the same information about reconciliation, mediation, judicial separation or a separation agreement as soon as he or she instructs a solicitor.

Both solicitors must certify that they have given their clients the required information before the case begins, otherwise the judge may adjourn the proceedings until the requirement has been fulfilled.

Even after the proceedings have started, if both spouses wish to attempt reconciliation at any stage, the judge will adjourn the proceedings – although if the talks break down, either spouse can ask the court to resume the case.

Even if the judge believes the couple can't be reconciled, he may still adjourn the case to give them a chance to come to some agreement on any of the outstanding issues, such as property, finances and children.

Any communication between the spouses – or with anyone else – aimed at trying to resolve the couple's differences may not be used in evidence if the case does go ahead.

Divorce proceedings may be brought in the High Court or the Circuit Family Court, although the Circuit Court must transfer the matter to the High Court on the application of any interested party if it concerns land with a rateable value of more than €254. (The Circuit Court may assess the rateable value of any land, which does not already have a rateable valuation.) The decision whether to bring proceedings in the Circuit Court or High Court is one of fundamental importance. It depends on a number of matters, including the value of the family's assets and the right of appeal, on which a family law solicitor is best placed to advise.

Proceedings are heard in private, generally in different courts (or on different days) from non-family law proceedings and are as informal as possible. Even though a couple may have applied for a divorce, the court has the power to grant a judicial separation or decree of nullity instead, though this would be unusual. A divorce may only be granted where four conditions are *all* fulfilled:

- the spouses have lived apart for at least four of the five years before proceedings were issued,

- there is no reasonable prospect of the couple being reconciled,

- *proper provision* must exist (or be made) for *both* spouses and any dependent children, and

- *either* spouse was domiciled in the State when proceedings began (or lived in the State for at least a year before that date).

Since 2001, Irish couples who are prepared to live abroad for a period may be able to circumvent the required four-year waiting period.

European Council Regulation 1347, introduced on March 1, 2001, covers the recognition and enforcement of judgements in matrimonial matters. The new regulation applies to civil proceedings relating to divorce, legal separation, nullity and child custody in the courts of every European Union State except Denmark.

Formerly, foreign divorces were only recognised in Ireland in certain circumstances. The 1986 Domicile and Recognition of Foreign Divorces Act allowed the recognition of a divorce granted anywhere in Britain and Northern Ireland as long as either spouse was domiciled there. In contrast, the new Regulation requires the Irish courts to recognise a British divorce which is granted on the basis of "habitual residence" in Britain or Northern Ireland. (The difference between the two terms is that 'domicile' implies an intention to live in a country permanently. 'Habitual residence' simply refers to the country where a person usually lives.)

In England and Wales, a spouse may petition for divorce after 12 months on the grounds of adultery or unreasonable behaviour. If both spouses agree, they may seek a divorce after two years' separation. If they don't agree, the separation must be five years or more. A person who had been habitually resident in England or Wales for one year would be entitled to bring an application for divorce. Once the English court accepted jurisdiction and agreed to deal with the matter, under the new regulation, the Irish courts would have to decline jurisdiction if the English divorce application were challenged by the other spouse. The Irish courts would also be required to recognise the English decree.

Living apart

The meaning of "living apart" was established in the case of *M. McA. v. X. McA.* (2000). The High Court ruled that, where a couple were living in the same household and one of them applied for a divorce, it was up to the court to decide whether the couple were in effect "living apart from one another" for the purpose of the Divorce Act.

Mr Justice McCracken said the matrimonial relationship could not be dictated purely by reference to the location of the couple or by whether they lived under the one roof. He said the court also had to consider the mental and intellectual attitude of the spouses. In this case, the couple had married in 1968 and had two children, both grown up. The wife claimed a decree of judicial separation. The husband counterclaimed for a decree of divorce, which was opposed by the wife.

In 1988, the husband left the family home when the wife discovered he was having an affair. In 1991, the husband ended his relationship and returned to live in the family home because, he said, he wanted to develop a better relationship with his son. The couple slept in separate bedrooms – even on holiday – and never resumed sexual relations. They had a "civilised relationship" at home, were polite to each other and would even take their meals together occasionally. The husband said he would tend to go early to his room – which he called his "apartment" – and watch television. He had a separate telephone line installed in his room. He would be away for three weekends out of four and would only see his wife for two or three hours a week.

In 1995, while the couple were still living in the same house, the wife had a sexual relationship with another man and, in 1996, the husband began a relationship with a woman with whom he was still living at the time of the court case. The husband finally left the family home in 1997. The judge said:

> "The fact that the section in effect allows the parties to live together for one year out of five and then separate again without affecting the rights under the section, seems to me to make it quite clear that it was the view of the legislature that it was necessary to make such provision, as otherwise parties who attempted but did not attain reconciliation would not be able to avail of the Act if they lived together for a short time during the preceding five years.

> "Marriage is not primarily concerned with where the spouses live or whether they live under the same roof, and indeed there can be a number of circumstances in which the matrimonial relationship continues even though the parties are not living under the same roof as, for example, where one party is in hospital or an institution of some kind, or is obliged to spend a great deal of time away from home in the course of his or her employment. Such separations do not necessarily constitute the persons as living apart from one another.

> "Clearly there must be something more than mere physical separation and the mental or intellectual attitude of the parties is also of considerable relevance. I do not think one can look solely either at where the parties physically reside, or at their mental or

intellectual attitude to the marriage. Both of these elements must be considered, and in conjunction with each other.

"Just as parties who are physically separated may in fact maintain their full matrimonial relationship, equally parties who live under the same roof may be living apart from one another. Whether this is so is a matter which can only be determined in the light of the facts of any particular case."

The judge said he was satisfied that, from the time the husband first left home in 1988, he considered the marriage at an end. When he returned in 1991, he did not intend to return to a marriage, but only wanted to have a better relationship with his children. The judge gave the wife the family home, an apartment in Tenerife, a business which she had been managing for many years, the neighbouring house and a house in Dublin. The husband was given the second home and the apartment in which he was living. The husband also paid £1.2 million for the wife's share of a joint business and was ordered to pay £4,500 a month maintenance and a lump sum of £300,000. The judge said the wife should also benefit from the husband's pension fund and life assurance policies.

Before the court decides whether or not to grant a divorce, it may make a number of temporary orders, including:

• an access order,

• a barring order,

• a child custody order,

• an interim barring order,

• a maintenance order,

• a protection order,

• a safety order, or

- an order preserving the family home, its contents or the proceeds from its sale.

If a spouse disposes of cash or property to try and prevent the other spouse obtaining his or her rightful share, the court may set aside such a transaction completed up to three years before the divorce application – even if the asset has been transferred out of the State. There is a presumption that any such disposal of property was intended to defeat the other spouse's claim, unless proved otherwise.

Once a divorce has been granted, the court may order one spouse to pay the other:

- a lump sum,

- maintenance, or

- secured maintenance

Maintenance payments may be secured against property, or the court may order that they be deducted at source from a spouse's salary – though the judge must take account of that spouse's views about whether he would make the payments without a so-called "attachment order". Alternatively payment may be made directly to the other spouse or through the District Court Clerk. All payments (other than pensions) are made without deducting income tax.

Maintenance payments may be backdated to the beginning of proceedings and the court may order that any retrospective payments (allowing for voluntary payments already made) be paid as a lump sum by a certain date. Alternatively, a spouse may be ordered to pay a lump sum towards the reasonable expenses of the other spouse before that spouse applied for maintenance.

Maintenance payments for a child cease when the child ceases to be dependent, or on the death of a spouse or dependent child. If the dependent spouse remarries, her own maintenance payments cease (except for any outstanding arrears).

The court may also enforce foreign maintenance orders. In the case of *McC. v. McC.* (1994), the defendant – an Irish citizen – married his wife in England in 1961 and divorced her in Hong Kong in 1986. The Hong Kong court had ordered him to pay maintenance but, in 1989, the defendant returned to Ireland, remarried and stopped the payments. The Circuit Court decided that the maintenance order could be enforced in Ireland. On appeal the High Court agreed, but said that, in enforcing foreign maintenance orders, the Irish courts had ample powers to ensure that no injustice resulted.

At any time after being granted a divorce, either spouse may ask the court to:

- transfer property from one spouse to the other (or in favour of a dependent child),

- settle any property for the benefit of the other spouse or any dependent child,

- vary any agreement or bequest settling property on either spouse or any dependent child, or

- reduce or extinguish the interest of either spouse under a settlement.

At any time after the court makes a secured maintenance, lump sum or property adjustment order, it may also order the sale of any property in which either spouse has an interest – although it won't order the sale of a family home where one spouse has been given the right of sole occupation.

The court may specify the conditions of sale of any property – including who should be offered the property and when – and may decide on the division of the sale proceeds. Any maintenance paid out of the sale proceeds ceases on the death or remarriage of the dependent spouse (except for any arrears due). Before making any such orders, the court must hear representations by anyone who has an interest in the property or the proceeds of its sale, such as a building society or bank.

If the court orders one divorcing spouse to transfer property to the other, stamp duty is not payable. The Divorce Act also makes special provision for the payment of capital gains tax, capital acquisitions tax and probate tax. The tax situation can be complicated after a divorce and the spouses' solicitors may recommend them to see a specialist tax accountant.

If the judge orders one of the spouses to sign over property and he or she fails to do so, the court may authorise someone else to sign the document on behalf of the defaulting ex-spouse.

When the court is considering the question of the family home, it must take into account that a couple cannot live together after a divorce and that dependent spouses and children need proper and secure accommodation. If a spouse has remarried and lives with a new partner, the court will not make an order affecting their home.

In the English case of *Cordle v. Cordle* (2001), the Court of Appeal said a judge should always look first at the housing needs of the spouses and provide a home for the primary carer and children. If there were enough assets available, he should then provide accommodation for the other parent. A court should also attempt to ensure that at least one of the parties could work and earn a living. Either spouse may also ask the court to make an order relating to:

- the exclusive right to live in the family home for life,

- the sale of the family home and division of the proceeds,

- the ownership of any property,

- dispensing with the consent of the other spouse to the sale of the family home,

- protection of the family home,

- arrears of rent or mortgage,

- restriction of the sale or disposal of household goods,

- partitioning of property,

- child welfare, custody and access, or

- a protection, safety, interim barring or barring order.

Normally both parents would remain joint guardians of their children after a divorce. However, the court may – after ordering probation, welfare or health board reports – declare that one parent is unfit to have custody and award custody to the other spouse. A parent who is declared unfit by the court will not have an automatic right to custody of the children if the other spouse dies. Among the reasons for being declared an unfit parent would be violence, mental or physical cruelty, sexual assault, desertion, alcoholism or serious mental illness.

The court may also give directions about access to dependent children and about their general welfare. This may involve supervised access by the non-custodial parent.

A divorced spouse may also ask the court at any time to make a *financial compensation order*, requiring the other spouse to take out a life insurance policy (or assign the benefit of an existing policy) to improve the financial security of the dependent spouse or children or to make up for her loss of a benefit such as a pension.

The court won't make such an order where the applicant has remarried, and the order ceases once the applicant dies or marries again. The court may also make a pensions' adjustment order.

If a divorced spouses dies without providing properly for a former spouse, the surviving spouse – if still single – may apply for a share of the estate of the deceased person. Normally, when granting a divorce, the court will also make an order preventing such an application in the future by one or both spouses.

The court won't grant a share in the estate if the surviving spouse had deserted the deceased spouse or had behaved in such a way that it would be unjust to give the survivor a share. (But a spouse who leaves the home because of intolerable behaviour by the other spouse may not be guilty of desertion.)

The personal representative of the deceased person (that is the executor or administrator of the estate) must make reasonable efforts to inform the surviving spouse of the death. If the survivor intends to apply (or has already applied) for a share of the estate, or an order has already been made in favour of the surviving spouse, that spouse must tell the personal representative within a month of being notified, otherwise the representative may distribute the assets regardless.

Any application for a share in an estate must usually be made within six months of a grant of probate or administration being taken out. The judge will hear evidence from any relevant person, including any new spouse. The court will also take into account any property adjustment, lump sum payment or bequest already made to the surviving spouse and will not give the survivor – in total – more than their legal right under the 1965 Succession Act: half the estate (or one third, if there are children).

When making orders under the Divorce Act, the court is bound to consider all the matters set out in section 20 of the Act, including the income, earning capacity, property and other financial resources of both spouses, as well as their financial needs, obligations and responsibilities (whether in the case of remarriage or not). It particularly has to look at:

• the family's former standard of living,

• the ages of the spouses,

• how long they were married or lived together,

- any physical or mental disability,

- the contribution which each spouse made to the welfare of the family, including any contribution made by looking after the home,

- the effect of marital responsibility on the earning capacity of either spouse, particularly the effect of staying home to care for the family,

- any income or social welfare benefits to which either spouse is entitled,

- the relevant conduct of both spouses (such as desertion),

- the accommodation needs of both spouses,

- the value of any benefit (such as a pension) which would be lost to one spouse because of the divorce, and

- the rights of anyone else, including a new husband or wife.

These matters have been considered in some detail by the High Court and Circuit Court, including cases where large sums of money were involved – such as *J.D. v. D.D.* (1997) and *M. McA. v. X. McA.* (2000).

Not every judge will give the same weight to every factor in section 20. Lord Justice Hoffman said in *Piglowska v. Piglowska* (1999):

> "There are many cases which involve value judgments ... on which reasonable people may differ. Since judges are also people, this means that some degree of diversity in their application of values is inevitable."

Section 20(2)(a) of the Divorce Act – which requires a judge to take note of any financial resources a spouse is "likely to have in the foreseeable future" – has been interpreted as allowing a judge to consider property which, strictly speaking, belongs to third parties.

In the English case of *Thomas v. Thomas* (1995), the Court of Appeal said a court did not have to limit its orders exclusively to resources of capital or income which were actually shown to exist. It might infer from the evidence that other, unidentified resources were available. The court said a judge need not totally disregard the potential availability of wealth from sources owned or administered by others.

In a similar case in Ireland, *F. v. F.* (2002), the main asset was the family home, which was built on land originally owned by the husband's father. The family stud farm was also on land owned by the husband's father. The wife claimed that her husband was the beneficial owner of these lands, and she should be entitled to a share in them.

Mr Justice O'Sullivan did not agree that he could make a property adjustment order in respect of the lands, but he said the husband's father was fully aware that the husband had developed the stud for his own benefit and that of his family. The judge said the husband could resist any claim by his father to the land, and it was unlikely that the father would take steps against his son. Accordingly, the judge said he should take into account the value of land adjoining the family home as an asset available to the husband.

Inheritances – or "interests in expectancy" – may also form part of the assets, which a judge will take into consideration.

The court also has to take account of any separation agreement still in force, as it did in the High Court case of *J.N. v. R.N.* (1999) and the Circuit Court case of *M.G. v. M.G.* (2000).

In relation to any dependent children, the court must take into account:

• their financial needs,

• their property or financial resources,

• any physical or mental disability,

- any income or social welfare benefits to which they are entitled,

- their accommodation needs,

- the parents' proposed education or training of the children,

- the financial circumstances of the parents, and

- any parental separation agreement.

The court may subsequently vary any order dealing with money or property in the light of changed circumstances or new evidence. The application may be made by either spouse, by a new spouse, or, on the death of a spouse, by anyone who has "a sufficient interest" or on behalf of a dependent child. Clearly this gives the court power to reduce maintenance – or even, in an extreme case, to order that property be handed back – if, for example, a remarried couple find themselves homeless or in financial difficulties because of the burden of maintenance payments.

The conduct of a spouse will be relevant in certain circumstances, such as where one has deserted the other or has behaved so badly that the other spouse has been forced to leave home. But the judge will disregard such conduct when making orders relating to maintenance payments for children.

In the case of *T. v. T.* (2002), the Supreme Court approved the decision of Lord Denning in *Wachtel v. Wachtel* (1973) that, short of misbehaviour which was 'obvious and gross', the court should not reduce an order for financial provision merely because of what was formerly regarded as guilt or blame. "To do so would be to impose a fine for supposed misbehaviour in the course of an unhappy married life," said Denning.

Earlier financial and property orders – made at the time of a divorce *a mensa et thoro* or a judicial separation – may be discharged if a spouse applies for a divorce. But if the orders are not discharged when the court grants a divorce, they remain in force.

In most family law cases, legal costs are not awarded, so each spouse has to foot his or her own legal bill. In the case of repeated applications to court and lengthy or complicated proceedings, these can run into tens of thousands of euros.

Division of assets

The law on the division of assets in Ireland differs from English law and common law. In England, in cases where there were extensive family assets and a "clean break" solution was considered desirable, the courts used to grant the wife a lump sum large enough to provide for her "reasonable requirements" until her death. The rest of the family assets went in general to the husband. This was the usual rule where a wife had been a stay-at-home wife and mother.

But the case of *White v. White* (2000) marked a turning point in the English approach to the division of matrimonial property in "big money cases".

The House of Lords said financial needs or "reasonable requirements" should not be regarded as the only factor in deciding an award, particularly when the couple's financial resources exceeded their needs. They particularly stressed the value of a woman's work in the home as a wife and mother.

The House of Lords said there should be no presumption that assets should be equally divided between spouses, but equality of division should be used as a yardstick against which the final division should be checked. The court should depart from equality only if there was good reason for doing so. The Lords said the courts were entitled to take into consideration that property had been acquired before marriage or had been inherited. The overall test in the division of assets was fairness all the circumstances, in particular in the light of the requirements of the statute.

The English courts were subsequently at pains to reiterate that *White v. White* did not introduce a requirement for equal division of assets. In *Cowan v. Cowan* (2002), Lord Justice Thorpe said the decision "clearly does not introduce a rule of equality. The yardstick of equality is a cross check against discrimination. Fairness is the rule." But the court ruled that if one spouse had made an exceptional contribution, that could justify a departure from the principle of equality.

In *W. v. W.* (2001), the Irish High Court approved the principles in *White v. White* (2001), but said that where assets were the proceeds of sale of an inherited property, that should be taken into account.

In that case, a wife had sought some of the proceeds of the sale of a farm which had been inherited by her husband. The couple were in their 50s and the wife had made a substantial contribution to the family as primary carer of the children. The court awarded a wife a lump sum of £4.7 million, giving her a total of £4.9 million out of total assets of approximately £17 million.

In the case of *K. v. K.* (2001), a High Court judge also adopted the principles in *White v. White* and said that he was "happy that, in current phraseology, the court may use the term 'equality'." He awarded the wife half the assets of her husband and his new partner, and the husband appealed to the Supreme Court.

The couple, who had married in England in 1963, had six children and separated in 1980. In 1982 they signed a deed of separation. The wife remained in the family home with the children, while the husband agreed to pay maintenance. A clause in the separation agreement allowed for variation of maintenance if there was a fundamental change in the circumstances of either spouse.

In 1995, the husband obtained a divorce in Haiti and went through a ceremony of marriage with M.B. in the United States. (He and M.B. married in a civil ceremony in Ireland in 2001 after his divorce.) After the separation, the husband obtained a very good job with a US company and became very rich – though most of his property was held jointly with

M.B. He was paid very well, and received a bonus of up to one hundred per cent of his salary.

The wife applied for a divorce in Ireland in 1998. In his judgment at the end of the five-day hearing in November 2000, the High Court judge criticised the husband as a man of "corporate mentality" whose attitude towards his wife was determined by "the questionable morality emanating from this mid-American company". The judge condemned the way the husband had obtained the Haitian divorce and remarried in the United States, and described him as having "driven a coach and four through Irish legislation". He said the marriage in the United States was bigamous.

The judge said he intended to adopt the fundamental rules that had been in existence for nearly 200 years in deciding whether a wife was entitled to be maintained according to the style of her husband. The judge ordered the husband to transfer the family home to the wife and pay her maintenance equal to half his annual salary (including bonuses) backdated to May 1999 and a lump sum of £1.5 million, representing about half the assets held by the husband and his new wife.

At a later hearing, the judge also ordered the trustees of the husband's Irish pension fund to pay 80% of the husband's Irish pension to the wife when it fell due. A counterclaim by the husband was dismissed and he was also ordered to pay his wife's costs, as well as his own. The husband appealed on the grounds that the High Court judge had failed to pay due regard to the 1982 separation deed or to the fact that the couple had been separated for more than 20 years.

The Supreme Court criticised the way the High Court judge had come to his decision. Mrs Justice Catherine McGuinness said:

> "While I would of course accept that the wife of a rich man (or the husband of a rich woman) could always expect a substantially greater award both in income and in capital than the parties to the average marriage,

I very much doubt that a policy of equal division of assets between husband and wife has prevailed under common law rules since the beginning of the 19th century, or even the 20th century, either in this jurisdiction or in England.

"The concept of a single capital payment to the wife to meet her 'reasonable requirements' for the remainder of her life has never in fact formed a part of Irish family law. There are two main reasons for this. Firstly, such a capital payment is inevitably a part of a 'clean break' settlement in divorce proceedings. In this jurisdiction the legislature has, in the Family Law (Divorce) Act 1996, laid down a system of law where a 'clean break' solution is neither permissible nor possible.

"Secondly, the approach of the Irish courts, in accordance with both Article 41.2 of the Constitution and the statutory guidelines, has been to give full credit to the wife's contribution through her work in the home and as a mother to her children. In this jurisdiction, the overriding requirement of a fair outcome is governed by Section 20(5) of the 1996 Act …

"The provisions of the 1996 Act leave a considerable area of discretion to the court in making proper financial provision for spouses in divorce cases. This discretion, however, is not to be exercised at large. The statute lays down mandatory guidelines.

"The court must have regard to all the factors set out in Section 20, measuring their relevance and weight according to the facts of the individual case. In giving the decision of the court, a judge should give reasons for the way in which his or her discretion has been exercised in the light of the statutory guidelines. In this case, the judge notably failed to do this."

The judge also said that, under section 20(3) of the Divorce Act, the court had to "have regard to the terms of any separation agreement which has been entered into by the spouses and is still in force."

The Supreme Court returned the matter to the High Court to consider the question of "proper provision" in the light of the mandatory provisions of the Divorce Act.

The meaning of the phrase "proper provision" was explained by the Supreme Court in *T. v. T*. That case involved a successful professional who left his wife after he had a series of affairs.

For some years after they married, the wife had worked as unofficial receptionist in the husband's practice, acted as secretary and furnished and cleaned his office. The wife, who had had seven pregnancies, said she felt "demeaned and ridiculed" when the husband admitted in 1996 that he was having an affair with a member of his staff.

The High Court estimated that the husband was worth between £14 million and £20 million. Most of his fortune was based on property which he bought after leaving his wife. His annual income was estimated at over £1 million.

In December 2001, the High Court granted the husband a divorce and ordered him to pay his wife a lump sum of £5 million. The husband had been paying £400 a week for maintenance of the couple's three children. The High Court ordered him to pay £800 a week to maintain the youngest boy.

The judge said the wife had been "appalled by the husband's behaviour" and the "anguish suffered by [the youngest child] was enormous". He had intended to give the wife 51 per cent of the husband's pension but, in the light of her husband's behaviour, he had increased this to 55 per cent. The husband was also ordered to pay his wife's legal costs.

The husband appealed to the Supreme Court against the size of the lump sum, the pension adjustment and the costs order. By a four-to-one majority, the appeal on the lump sum and costs was dismissed. The pension appeal was allowed.

Counsel for the husband said the wife should have received less than £5 million because:

(1) she could return to court at any time because of the lack of finality in Irish divorce law;

(2) she had her own income and earning capacity;

(3) at the time of the separation, the husband had transferred to her a third of his assets, worth £1.5 million;

(4) 80% of the husband's assets were acquired in the two years after the separation;

(5) she did not have exceptional needs, the children were substantially provided for and the husband had new obligations; and

(6) her standard of living before the separation could be achieved with less than £5 million.

On behalf of the wife, counsel argued that:

(1) the court should apply the statutory criteria set out in the Divorce Act;

(2) the traditional role of women in the home should not be valued at less than the role of the breadwinner;

(3) the assets should be assessed at the date of trial, except where there was deliberate or reckless wastage; and

(4) the lack of a maintenance order for the wife should be reflected by payment of a large lump sum.

Chief Justice Ronan Keane said that in "big money" cases – which he preferred to call "ample resources" cases – equal division of the assets was "emphatically not mandated by the [Irish] legislation." Provided that was borne in mind, he thought there should be no difficulty with the Irish courts adopting a broadly similar approach to *White v. White*.

Mrs Justice Susan Denham, giving another of the majority verdicts in the Supreme Court, said the Divorce Act did not seek to establish a fault system and the court should not have reduced the husband's share of his pension just because of what was formerly regarded as guilt or blame. "To do so would be to impose a fine for supposed misbehaviour in the course of an unhappy married life," she said.

Judge Denham said the High Court was correct to value the husband's assets at the date of trial, since that was consistent with the wording of the statute. However, the fact that a spouse had acquired a considerable sum of money after separation, the basis for the acquisition or the existence of a deed of separation might be very relevant.

In this case, the husband's assets had benefited greatly from the increase in property prices, but the funding of the property was assisted by his legal practice, which had benefited directly from the wife's work as receptionist and cleaner and, indirectly, by her as the home-maker.

The judge said the Divorce Act provided for "proper provision, not division," and it was not a question of dividing the assets on a basis of percentage – though a figure of one third of the assets might be a "useful benchmark to fairness."

She added:

> "'Proper provision' is a proper provision based on the constitutional and statutory recognition of the family. The special place of the family and of family duties are recognised. The court must look at both aspects of a spouse's role in the family, two sides of the coin. Thus the court must have regard to the role of the spouses in relation to the welfare of the family, to their contribution in looking after the home or caring for the family.

> "On the other side of the coin, the court must have regard to the effect on the earning capacity of each of

the spouses of the marital responsibilities assumed by each, and the degree to which the future earning capacity of a spouse was impaired by reason of the spouse having relinquished or foregone the opportunity of remunerative activity in order to look after the home or care for the family.

"A long-lasting marriage, especially in the primary childbearing and rearing years of a woman's life, carries significant weight, especially if the wife has been the major home and family carer.

"The concepts of certainty and consistency are subject to the necessity of fairness. Consequently, each case must be considered on its own facts, in light of the principles set out in the law, so as to achieve a just result. Thus, while the underlying constitutional principle is one of making proper provision for the spouses and children, this is to be administered with justice to achieve fairness."

The judge said the High Court had not failed to consider the income and earning capacity of the wife, but it would help if such factors were considered "in an express manner, and reasons for decisions given".

Judge Denham said the absence of a 'clean break' principle in Irish law did not exclude a lump sum order, and payment of a lump sum could bring "a fair financial decision and certainty to the financial affairs of the family."

Until now, judges have maintained that Irish divorce legislation does not permit a "clean break" because, under the statutes, divorced couples can return to court to ask for variations in financial and property orders.

Mrs Justice Catherine McGuinness said in the case of *J.D. v. D.D.* (1998):

"The Oireachtas has made it clear that a 'clean break'

situation is not to be sought and that, if anything, financial finality is virtually to be prevented.

"The court, in making virtually any order in regard to finance and property on the breakdown of a marriage, is faced with the situation where finality is not and never can be achieved. This also appears to mean that no agreement on property between the parties can be completely final, since such finality would be contrary to the policy and provisions of the legislation.

"The statutory policy is, therefore, totally opposed to the concept of the 'clean break'. This policy is not only clear on the face of the statutes but was most widely discussed, referred to and advocated in the considerable debate that surrounded the enactment of divorce legislation."

But financial finality in divorce may not be so far away, following the *T. v. T.* decision. The Chief Justice, Mr Justice Ronan Keane, accepted that, in some cases "finality is not possible" and that the legislation "expressly provides for the variation of custody and access orders and of the level of maintenance payments."

But he added that he did not believe that the Oireachtas intended that the courts should abandon any possibility of achieving certainty and finality and of avoiding further litigation between ex-spouses. "I am satisfied that, while the Irish legislation is careful to avoid going as far as the English legislation in adopting the 'clean break' approach – not least because of the Constitutional constraints – it is not correct to say that the legislation goes so far as virtually to prevent financial finality," he said. "On no view could such an outcome be regarded as desirable and I am satisfied that it is most emphatically not mandated by the legislation under consideration."

European Council Regulation 1347 could also have implications for property rights. While Irish courts have the power to reopen financial matters, and a spouse does not have the legal right to contract out of future variations of maintenance, in England, all financial matters may be finalised once and for all on the granting of a divorce.

Divorce Questionnaire

It would be helpful if you completed this questionnaire before your first consultation with a solicitor.

  (i) Your full name, address and date of birth.

 (ii) Your spouse's full name, address and date of birth.

(iii) Your occupation and your spouse's occupation.

(iv) Date and place of marriage. (Please produce your state marriage certificate.) Are you satisfied that the marriage was valid?

 (v) Names and dates of birth of any children. Is any of them still under 18, receiving full-time education or suffering from physical or mental disability?

(vi) Are you both Irish citizens? Are you domiciled here or have you both been ordinarily resident in Ireland for more than one year?

(vii) What date did you separate? Give a full list of the addresses at which you and your spouse have lived since you parted and whether the properties were rented or owned by either of you.

(viii) Detail ALL residences owned by you or your spouse. In whose names are the properties registered? What is the value of each property? Give full details of any outstanding loans or mortgages.

(ix) Does either of you own any other land or premises?

(x) What are your respective incomes? Provide details of your assets, debts and pensions.

(xi) Have there been previous family law proceedings of any type? Give details with copies of any previous court orders or separation agreement.

(xii) Why has the marriage broken down? Who was to blame? Has there been unreasonable behaviour, violence or cruelty (mental or physical)? If so, give details and approximate dates. Bring any diary or notes with you. Has either spouse deserted the family home?

(xiii) Is there any reasonable prospect of a reconciliation between you and your spouse? Have you considered counselling or mediation?

Chapter Nine

Children

One of the most heartrending aspects of separation or divorce can be the fate of the children. The parents may hate the sight of one another, but both may love their children and wish to have custody – that is living with the children and having the day-to-day control of them. One parent may also wish to deny any access, or contact with the children, to the other, but the courts will seldom agree to this.

If a couple divorce or obtain a judicial separation, the court will always make orders relating to the children, including orders for custody and access. While very young children will often be left with their mother, fathers have a right (and duty) to see their children regularly and to help with their upbringing.

The 1964 Guardianship of Infants Act was the first major piece of legislation in modern times to address the question of children's welfare after marriage breakdown. The first principle of the Act was that the child's welfare should be the paramount consideration. The Act gave married parents joint guardianship of their children and allowed the court to appoint a guardian if necessary. The legislation provided for court orders on child maintenance, custody and access.

Guardianship involves the collective rights and duties of a parent towards a child. It includes the duty to maintain and properly care for the child, as well as the right to make decisions about the child's religious and secular education, health needs and other matters affecting the child's welfare. The 1964 Act provides for:

- the welfare of the child to be paramount,
- joint guardianship of both parents,
- court orders for custody, access and maintenance, and
- "fit person" orders.

The first consideration of any court is the welfare of the children. In *G. v. An Bord Uchtála* (1980), the Chief Justice said a child had a right "to be fed and to live, to be reared and educated, to have the opportunity of working and of realising his or her full personality and dignity as a human being."

"Welfare" is defined as the child's "religious, moral, intellectual, physical and social" welfare. Normally, a child's religious welfare would be safeguarded by ensuring that the person who had custody of the child was of the same faith. But in *Cullen v. Cullen* (1970), the court accepted that a woman who had lapsed from the practice of her religion would ensure that her son would be taught religion and say his prayers.

In the past, the moral welfare of a child required that he should not be brought up in an adulterous relationship, but this has changed. In *J.W. v. B.W.* (1971), the court awarded custody to a father because the mother was living in an adulterous relationship with a man who had deserted his own wife and children. The Chief Justice said a "more unhealthy abode for the three children would be hard to imagine."

Conversely, in *J.C. v. O.C.* (1980), the President of the High Court refused a father custody because he was in an adulterous relationship and the children were sufficiently well-educated by the mother.

In *MacD. v. MacD.* (1979), the President of the High Court granted custody to the father because he said the wife was an adulteress. The Supreme Court, by a two to one majority, said the children's welfare (not the parents' behaviour) was the first concern.

But in *S. v. S.* (1992), the Chief Justice said that the conduct of parents was only relevant insofar as affected the welfare of the child. And in the case of *G. v. An Bord Uchtála* (1980), the judge said that, while the welfare of the child was to be "paramount," it was not the sole consideration.

In *C.C. v. P.C.* (1994), the court said the word "welfare" must be taken in its widest sense, and it wasn't just a question of "totting up the marks which might be awarded under each of the five headings."

A court's decision on custody can be swayed by the age of the child. In *O'D. v. O'D.* (1979), the judge said that children of "tender years" were better in a mother's custody.

The 1997 Children Act allows a court to award custody jointly to the father and mother but Mrs Justice Catherine McGuinness said in *E.P. v. C.P.* (1998) that joint custody could not work satisfactorily if there was a high level of conflict between the parents, or where they could not work together sensible and happily in the interests of the children.

Sometimes, however, awarding custody to one parent can worsen the hostility between them. In the case of *D. O'S. v. C.A.* (1999), the same judge awarded joint custody to two unmarried parents in the hope that caring for their child might help them put their antagonisms behind them.

A parent who remains a guardian but does not have custody of a child is entitled to apply for access. Such an order may be varied at any time in the interests of the child. Even where a father might be violent (as in *A. MacB. v. A. MacB.* (1984)) or a potential abuser (as in *O'D. v. O'D.* (1994)), a court will try to ensure that children can continue to see their father, albeit in circumstances where the visits are supervised.

The 1997 Children Act allows any relative of the child to apply to the court for leave to seek access. The court will take into account the applicant's connection with the child, the risk of disruption to the child's life and the wishes of the child's guardians.

Every case is looked at individually and case law is therefore only a guide to what the courts might decide in a particular instance.

The court may make whatever order it considers proper in relation to guardianship, custody or maintenance of a child, and may order the father or mother to make "reasonable payments." (The order can be made when the couple are living together, but it won't take effect unless they separate.)

A guardian normally has the right to custody of the child (unless a court decides otherwise). The mother and father of a child are its joint guardians, but the definition of "father" in the 1964 Act excludes the unmarried father of a child.

In *K. v .W.* (1991), W had become pregnant by K. She wanted to give the baby up for adoption, while he wanted to keep it himself. The Circuit Court gave the father custody. The High Court judge referred the matter to the Supreme Court for its construction of the 1964 Act. The Supreme Court said an unmarried father had a right to apply for guardianship, but no right to be appointed guardian. The child's welfare was paramount and the Act equalised the rights of children, not of parents.

The case was sent back to the High Court, where the judge held against the father. He said the welfare of the child was better served by being adopted and thus become a member of a family, as recognised by the Constitution. (K. eventually won in the European Court of Human Rights, but the child stayed with the adoptive parents.)

Even if parents behave badly towards one another, they still have a natural, statutory and Constitutional right to be the guardians of their own children. In *Western Health Board v. An Bord Uchtála* (1995), a husband sought custody of his natural child. He had been separated from his wife, who was having an affair with another man. The husband forced his wife to have intercourse in 1988 and she became pregnant. Although she believed her lover was the child's father, she registered her husband as the father on the birth certificate and gave her daughter up for adoption.

The husband refused to consent to the adoption and, two years later, agreed to a blood test that proved he was the child's father. In 1992, when the child had been with its adoptive parents for more than three years, the father brought proceedings for custody of the child.

The Supreme Court refused to confirm the adoption order and said that, just because a parent had failed in his duty to his child and that failure was likely to continue until the child was 18, did not mean that he had abandoned all his parental rights.

But the court said that its refusal to allow the child to be adopted did not affect the issue of custody, where the child's welfare had to be the paramount consideration.

The 1964 Guardianship of Infants Act was updated in 1987 by the Status of Children Act, which equalised the status of legitimate and illegitimate children. It also addressed the question of the rights and duties of single fathers. The more important effects of the Act were to:

- abolish the concept of illegitimacy,

- allow a child born of a voidable marriage to retain its legitimate status,

- give unmarried fathers legal rights to be appointed guardian or to seek custody and/or access,

- allow payments of birth and funeral expenses to the mother by the father,

- amend the Maintenance Act to allow payments by a father,

- allow a father (or child) to apply for a declaration of paternity,

- provide for blood tests to prove paternity, and

- allow a presumption of paternity where a baby was born in a subsisting marriage within 10 months, or if the father's name was on the Birth Register.

In *J.P.D. v. M.G.* (1990), a man sought custody of two children, but his divorced wife said they weren't his and demanded a blood test. The High Court ordered a test on the basis that the importance of truth and justice outweighed the presumption of the children's legitimacy.

The husband appealed, claiming that the children's welfare was paramount and that he was presumed to be their guardian, as they were conceived within marriage. The Supreme Court unanimously agreed that the children's welfare should always be the primary concern and that a judge should use his discretion in ordering a blood test. But in this case, they said a test should be ordered, and they dismissed the appeal.

Occasionally a parent who loses custody may decide to breach the court order by removing a child from the jurisdiction. But the 1991 Child Abduction and Enforcement of Custody Orders Act allows courts in some countries to enforce custody orders made here, and *vice versa*.

The purpose of the Act was clearly spelled out by an English judge in *P. v. P. (Minors) (Child Abduction)* (1992):

> "Its underlying assumption is that the courts of all its signatory countries are equally capable of ensuring a fair hearing to the parties and a skilled and humane evaluation of the issues of child welfare involved. Its underlying purpose is to ensure stability for children, by putting a brisk end to the efforts of parents to have their children's future decided where they want and when they want, by removing them from their country of residence to another jurisdiction chosen arbitrarily by the absconding parent."

The Act came into force on October 1, 1991 and deals only with wrongful retention *after* that date. The Act includes two schedules: the Hague Convention (dealing with breach of the custody rights which are currently being exercised) and the Luxembourg Convention (dealing with improper removal of children across an international frontier, including failure to return a child after access). The Act:

• sets up a Central Authority,

• gives the court *interim* powers,

• allows the court to refuse to return a child, and

• increases Garda powers.

The Hague Convention applies to children under 16 who normally lived in the contracting state before the breach. The Convention:

• establishes custody rights,

• sets up a Central Authority in each State,

• requires the immediate co-operation of the Central Authority,

• sets a one-year time limit for any initial request (though late applications are not debarred),

• allows the court to refuse to return the child if his human rights or fundamental freedoms would be affected, and

• allows a derogation if:
  (1) The applicant was not exercising custody rights,
  (2) the applicant had agreed to the removal,
  (3) there would be a grave risk of physical or psychological harm to the child, or
  (4) the child objected.

The Luxembourg Convention defines *child* as a person under 16 of any nationality.

The main differences between the two Conventions are:

• the Hague Convention does *not* require a prior court order,

• the Luxembourg Convention covers breach of access,

- the time limits, and

- the reasons for refusal to return a child – which are discretionary in the Hague Convention, but technical in the Luxembourg Convention.

In *L.R. v. D.R.* (1992), an Irish woman had decided not to return to her American husband in the USA with their two children in 1991. The husband was granted custody in the USA in 1992. The Irish Department of Justice said the convention only dealt with wrongful retention after October 1991, but the Irish court said it had jurisdiction, as the children were within the State. Their welfare required that they stay with the mother and that took precedence over the convention.

In *J. v. R.* (1993), the daughter of an unmarried English couple had been made a ward of court in England in 1990. The mother brought the child to Ireland in 1992 and the father applied for her return. The mother claimed that the child was of "tender years" and her religious welfare would be affected by her return, as the father wasn't a Catholic. But the Chief Justice said an unmarried father also had rights under the 1987 Act, and the Luxembourg Convention provided for unqualified enforcement of child custody orders. He ordered the mother to take the child back to England.

But unmarried fathers may not always have the same rights as married fathers under the Hague Convention. In *H.I. v. M.G.* (1999), the Supreme Court said:

> "It is clear ... that the rights of unmarried fathers under the (Hague) Convention present particular difficulties, given the unique relationship of the natural father to his children and the fact that in a number of jurisdictions, including our own, they do not have any automatic rights to custody equivalent to those of married parents.

> "However, the appropriate method of addressing diffi-

culties of that nature which may arise in the operation
of conventions on private international law is through
the machinery of special commissions in The Hague
which regularly monitor and review the operation of
conventions in the contracting states, rather than by
innovative judicial responses to admittedly difficult
cases in which upholding the convention as enacted
may give rise to what seems a harsh or inequitable
result."

Even when the child's best interests may be served by
remaining in Ireland, the courts here may order the child's
return to another jurisdiction. In *P.S.S. v. J.A.S.* (1994), an
Irish woman, who was divorcing her American husband,
brought their young daughter to Ireland in breach of a ruling
by the Los Angeles Superior Court. The husband asked the
Irish High Court to order the return of the child.

In the High Court, the judge said that, although he believed
it would be in the child's best interests to stay with her mother
and grandparents in Ireland, the Hague Convention required
that the girl be returned to California. The judge didn't believe
this would expose the child to physical or psychological harm
and he ordered that the husband should pay for his wife to
take the child back to America, where she would remain in
the mother's custody pending the outcome of the Californian
court case.

The following day, the mother handed the child over to
the father, in defiance of the High Court order. The judge
then ordered that the child should stay with her paternal
grandmother in America pending the order of the Californian
court.

The constitutionality of the 1991 Act was challenged in
Wadda v. Ireland (1994). In that case, the wife, who was an
Irish citizen, married a Moroccan. They lived in the United
Kingdom and had one daughter. When the marriage broke
down, the wife returned to Ireland with her daughter and

began proceedings to be appointed sole guardian of the child. The husband asked the Irish courts to order the return of the girl to the United Kingdom.

The Irish judge agreed that the husband was entitled to an order returning the child, but he deferred the implementation of the decision while the mother challenged the constitutionality of the Act.

The wife said the Act was unconstitutional because it deprived her of the right of custody and access, displaced the jurisdiction of the Irish courts and failed to protect the rights of the family.

The judge said Article 20 of the Hague Convention gave the Irish courts jurisdiction to refuse to return the child unless her human rights and fundamental freedoms were protected – and this included the rights in Articles 40 to 44 of the Irish Constitution.

But the judge said that, where the courts were requested to return a child to a country, which was not a signatory to the Convention, such as in the case of *L.R. v. D.R.*, it *could* first inquire into the welfare of the children.

If a court makes a custody order for a child, any application relating to the abduction of that child must be made to the same court. In *C. v. B.* (1995), an unmarried couple living in Ireland had a baby girl. Two months later, the mother took the child to live in England. The father applied for and was granted custody of the child by Castlebar District Court.

The High Court ordered the return of the child under the Luxembourg Convention and the mother appealed. The Supreme Court said that, since the District Court had made the custody order, it should also have made the order under the 1991 Act. The High Court had no jurisdiction to do so.

Even where one parent is awarded custody, both parents remain joint guardians and are entitled to a say in the upbringing of the children. Unsatisfactory access arrangements may be improved by further application to the court, but judges will look very disapprovingly on a parent who takes the law into his own hands by breaching a custody order. Almost invariably, the children will be traced and returned to the original parent, and the offending spouse may find himself further restricted in his access to the children.

The child of married parents may not be removed from the country by one parent, as both parents are entitled to custody under Irish law, unless a court makes an order to the contrary. In *H.I. v. M.G.* (1999), the Supreme Court said:

> "Married parents are entitled to the custody of the children without any court order or formal legal agreement to that effect, and the removal by one parent of the child or children to another jurisdiction without the consent of the other will clearly constitute a wrongful removal … unless the rights were not being actually exercised at the time of the removal.

> "Even where the parent, or some other person or body concerned with the care of the child, is not entitled to custody, whether by operation of law, judicial or administrative decision or an agreement having legal effect, but there are proceedings in being to which he or it is a party and he or it has sought the custody of the child, the removal of the child to another jurisdiction while the proceedings are pending would, absent any legally excusing circumstances, be wrongful in terms of the Convention."

Chapter Ten

The Family Home

One of the biggest problems facing couples whose marriages break down is what happens to the family home. The issue of the family home – and, in Ireland, of the family farm – is at the centre of many of the legal disputes that follow a marriage breakdown. The issue came to the fore in 1986 when the electorate rejected the introduction of divorce, largely because of husbands' fears about the family farm being taken over by their former wives.

The Government attempted to reassure voters by introducing new laws and, in 1993, produced draft legislation to deal with the issue. The controversial Matrimonial Home Bill was referred to the Supreme Court by President Mary Robinson to test its constitutionality.

The Bill said that, where a dwelling (including a boat or a caravan!) had been occupied by a married couple at any time since June 25, 1993 and either spouse already had an interest in the property, the equitable interest in the property would belong to both spouses as joint tenants unless the 'owning spouse' declared in writing after separate legal advice that the Act did not apply. That meant that, if for example a man who owned his own home married a woman on June 24, 1993 and she moved into his house, she would effectively become half-owner in the property as soon as the Bill became law. (This didn't apply where the spouses already owned the home in equal shares.)

A homeowner could apply to court for a ruling that the law should not apply in his (or her) case and the other spouse could waive the right after legal advice. But, in the absence of any other agreement between the couple, all household goods (including furniture, bedding, linen, china, earthenware, glass, books and pets!) would also belong equally to the two spouses. Not surprisingly, the Supreme Court ruled in 1994 that the Bill was unconstitutional.

Article 41.3.1° of the Constitution says: "The State pledges itself to guard with special care the institution of marriage, on which the family is founded, and to protect it against attack."

The Attorney General argued that the proposed legislation supported marriage and the family by securing the home for the family, emphasising the partnership in marriage, favouring wives who worked at home and providing security for spouses and children in the case of marriage breakdown.

But counsel assigned to challenge the validity of the Bill said the blanket and universal creation of a joint tenancy for both spouses in the family home constituted a clear failure by the state to protect the authority of the family. He said that quite clearly it was up to the spouses jointly to decide who owned the matrimonial home and in what shares. The automatic cancellation of that decision was a quite impermissible invasion into the authority of the family.

The court agreed that the institutions of marriage and the family would be strengthened if joint ownership of the family home could be *encouraged* by appropriate means, but it said a couple had the right under Article 41.1.1° of the Constitution to make their own decision about the family home, without the interference of the Oireachtas. The Bill interfered with that right – whether or not the joint decision was oppressive or unfair to either of them.

The court said the Bill also disregarded the date of purchase of the house. Decisions could have been made years before, with other property arrangements made on the basis of those decisions. The Bill could lead to a situation where one spouse, who had been "content though not enthusiastic" about the previous arrangement, would unreasonably refuse to waive the right to a half share, leading to litigation by the other spouse.

In some instances, the effect of the proposals would be automatically to cancel a joint decision freely made by both spouses as part of the authority of the family. This did not constitute "reasonably proportionate intervention" by the state with the rights of the family.

The Supreme Court said: "(We are) not … satisfied that the potentially indiscriminate alteration of what must be many joint decisions validly made within the authority of the family concerning the question of the ownership of the family home could reasonably be justified, even by such an important aspect of the common good."

The judges said it was not their job to decide which sections of the Bill were unconstitutional. If one section fell, the whole measure fell, so the court ruled that the entire Bill was unconstitutional.

The common law concept of marriage involved a duty by the husband to provide accommodation for his wife – even if she was separated from him. A wife might have had a right to prevent her husband mortgaging or selling the home in which she lived, even if he owned it. But those rights did not bind a third party who bought a family home in good faith, even without the wife's consent. In other words, if a husband sold the family home and the purchaser bought it in good faith, the sale would be valid, even if the wife had not consented beforehand.

Where homes are owned by one spouse alone, it is almost always the man. In the case of marital disputes, the husband could sell up his house and disappear with the proceeds. The 1976 Family Home Protection Act was the first major piece of legislation to deal with this problem.

The Minister for Justice told the Dáil that the main purpose of the 1976 Act was to prevent a vindictive spouse selling the family home over the heads of other family members. It also gave the courts power to prevent a spouse removing and selling furniture or other belongings.

Mr Justice Richard Johnson, in the case of *Bank of Ireland v. Slevin* (1995), said the purpose of the Act was to protect the family home and "to prevent families being evicted when a spouse, through either stupidity or greed or whatever else – or bad business or bad luck – lost the family home."

In a strictly legal sense, the person whose name is on the title deeds of a property has legal ownership, while a spouse whose name is not on the title deeds might have what is known as an equitable interest under the provisions of the 1995 Family Law Act and the Divorce Act.

Traditionally, a husband – as the wage-earner – may have bought a property in his sole name and paid the mortgage himself. Even if his wife contributed to the other running costs of the home, or paid for the improvement of the house or building of an extension, she would not have a legal right to the property.

Wives who stay at home, giving their husbands the opportunity to go out and earn money, undoubtedly make a contribution towards the home, but that contribution was not recognised in terms of ownership until the case of *L. v. L.* (1992). In that case, Mr Justice Robert Barr said that Article 41 of the Constitution enabled the court to take into account the "money's-worth" contribution of mothers who stayed at home to rear the family. But the Supreme Court unanimously overturned that judgment on the grounds that this was a new legal right, which could only be created by legislation.

The Oireachtas obliged with the 1989 Judicial Separation and Family Law Reform Act which allows a court, when making a property adjustment order, to take into account the contribution made by a spouse who looks after the home or cares for the family. That provision is mirrored in the 1995 Family Law Act and the Divorce Act.

Under the Family Home Protection Act, if the family home is sold by one spouse – who may be the legal owner of the property – without the written consent of the other spouse, the transaction is void. Anyone buying unregistered property formerly had to check every conveyance of the land after 1976, as a transaction that failed to comply with the law might have meant the property did not belong to its apparent owner. But the 1995 Family Law Act says a conveyance will be valid unless declared void by a court. Any proceedings to declare a conveyance void must be instituted within six years of the transaction. (This procedure is not necessary with registered land, as an entry in the register is regarded as proof of the title of the registered owner.)

Sometimes couples agree to sell their home and then want to back out of the sale for some reason. But in *Nestor v. Murphy* (1979) the court decided that, where spouses were co-owners of the home and they both agreed to sell it, they couldn't wriggle out of the deal just because the wife did not give her prior consent in writing.

No written consent is needed for a court to grant a *judgment* mortgage. In the case of *Containercare v. Wycherley* (1982), a husband and wife were joint owners of the family home. A creditor obtained a judgment mortgage against the husband for outstanding debts, and the mortgage was registered against the husband's share of the home, so that, in this case, the wife and the creditor effectively became joint owners of the property.

It is important, however, to realise that the 1976 Act does not, however, confer any right of ownership on the spouse whose consent is required.

The term "family home" was defined in the case of *National Irish Bank v. Graham* (1995), where the Supreme Court said that the definition of a "family home" was restricted to the precise terms of the Family Home Protection Act 1976, that is "primarily a dwelling in which a married couple ordinarily reside." It also means "a dwelling in which a spouse whose protection is in issue ordinarily resides" – or, if that spouse has left the other spouse, where he or she ordinarily used to reside. It may not include a holiday home or a house into which a couple have not yet moved. The court said judges could not extend that definition.

In the case of *B.M.C. v. P.J.C.* (1983), the judge said the court would not allow the owner of a family home to evade the law by transferring it into the name of a company controlled by one of the spouses, and then occupying the home under licence from the company.

In an effort to tie down the meaning of a family home, the 1995 Family Law Act defines a dwelling as "any building or part of a building occupied as a separate dwelling, and includes any garden or other land usually occupied with the dwelling, being land that is subsidiary and ancillary to it, is required for amenity or convenience and is not being used or developed primarily for commercial purposes, and includes a structure that is not permanently attached to the ground and a vehicle, or vessel, whether mobile or not, occupied as a separate dwelling."

That definition suggests that a farmhouse could be a family home, but the farmlands would not. Such clarification was needed because of the contentious issue, in the Irish context, as to whether the family farm constitutes a family home, under the Act.

In *AIB v. Austin and Susan O'Neill* (1995), Mrs O'Neill deposited the land certificate for a 63-acre farm in Co Carlow as an equitable mortgage against a loan of £50,000, without the prior written consent of Mr O'Neill. The bank obtained a court judgment for £48,000 and – while it accepted that it could not seize the couple's house and gardens – claimed it had an equitable mortgage over the rest of the land.

The High Court said the legislature clearly intended that the family home might form only part of a larger holding and the Act only required the prior written consent of the other spouse in relation to the home, not to the rest of the land. The judge ruled that the mortgage was valid against the farmlands, but not against the house and gardens.

In the UK, the House of Lords ruled in *Barclay's Bank v.*

O'Brien (1993) that a transaction was not invalidated just because a wife did not fully understand it – although where a person signed a document under duress or through misrepresentation, the transaction would not be valid.

But, in the case of *Bank of Ireland v. Michael and Una Smyth* (1995), the Supreme Court ruled that a person had to be properly informed in order to consent to a charge over the family home.

In 1978, Mrs Smyth had agreed to mortgage of the 124-acre family farm in Co Tipperary and signed a form under the 1976 Act consenting to the mortgage. Ten years later the couple owed £180,000 and in 1993 the bank asked the High Court for an order of possession, which was refused. Mrs Smyth said the bank never explained to her that she would lose her home if the mortgage payments were not made.

The Supreme Court said the bank did not have a duty to explain the mortgage fully to Mrs Smyth or to advise her to take independent legal advice. But it should have done so, to obtain good title to the land. In the circumstances, Mrs Smyth's uninformed consent was invalid and the mortgage agreement was void.

In *Bank of Ireland v. Hanrahan* (1987), a couple claimed that a mortgage was void because the wife had not given her consent until two hours *after* her husband deposited the title deeds with the bank. The judge said the mortgage was valid because there had been an implied agreement that the bank would only hold the deeds as custodian until the wife gave her consent.

General written consent to all future loans is now covered by an amendment to the 1976 Act by the 1995 Family Law Act. This may mean that, once a general written consent is given by one spouse, the other spouse may thereafter secure any future borrowings against the family home, effectively contracting out of the safeguards of the original legislation. This makes it all the more vital that the non-owning spouse take independent legal advice before signing any form of consent.

In *Mary O'Keeffe v. Brian Russell and AIB* (1994), Mr and Mrs O'Keeffe sold their 111-acre farm in Cork in 1978 and bought a 206-acre farm in Limerick for £700,000. They borrowed the deposit from the AIB and the couple's solicitor, Mr Russell, promised to lodge the land certificate of the new farm with the bank. He also promised to lodge the proceeds of sale of the Cork farm in a joint account.

But the money from the Cork farm was lodged in the sole name of Mr O'Keeffe and the bank made the loan for the new farm to him alone. Mrs O'Keeffe refused to accept joint responsibility for her husband's debt. In 1980, she left him and told the solicitor not to lodge the land certificate with the bank. He said he was bound to do so, and lodged the certificate.

Eventually Mr O'Keeffe fell behind in his loan payments and in 1982 the bank obtained a judgment against him. The farm was sold and most of the proceeds used to pay off Mr O'Keeffe's debt. The High Court ruled that the bank had no charge over Mrs O'Keeffe's share of the farm and the bank appealed.

The Supreme Court rejected the appeal and said Mrs O'Keeffe had not been party to the loan contract because it was not a joint loan, so there was no mortgage on her half of the farm.

A more straightforward case was *Bank of Ireland v. Slevin* (1995) where the bank claimed quarter of a million pounds from farmer Harry Slevin. The deeds of Mr Slevin's farm were deposited with the bank in 1977 as security for a loan, but Mrs Slevin had not consented in writing to the deposit. Mr Slevin claimed the whole mortgage was void for lack of consent, but the judge ruled that the mortgage was only void in relation to the family home, and he granted a charge over the rest of the farm.

If a spouse deserts the home or refuses to agree to its sale for reasons of malevolence, stubbornness or mental illness, the other spouse may apply to the court for an order dispensing with the need for that spouse's consent. But a dispensation is not retrospective and must be obtained *before* any sale.

A co-owning spouse who wants to separate, sell the home and divide the proceeds with the other spouse, may apply to the court for an order for sale in lieu of partition, as no purchaser is likely to want to buy a half share of the house and become a co-owner with the remaining spouse! The Partition Act 1868 says the court *shall* order the sale, unless it sees good reason to the contrary.

If a spouse deliberately engages in conduct which may lead to the loss of the home or make it unsuitable to live in, with the intention of depriving the dependent spouse or children of their home, the court may make "such order as it considers proper." If the home has already been lost or rendered uninhabitable, the court may order the spouse to pay compensation. But this section does not apply to a spouse whose behaviour, although immature or foolish, is not intended to deprive the other spouse of the family home.

Occasionally ownership of the family home is apparently held by third parties through off-shore trusts, often based in tax havens such as the Isle of Man or the Channel Islands. The rules of natural justice and the statutory requirements mean that these "owners" must be put on notice of any claims for property transfers or declarations of beneficial interest. Since they are outside the jurisdiction, it is not easy to compel them to obey Irish court orders. Without their co-operation, it may be impossible to achieve discovery of documents, and lawyers may be left relying on limited public records.

Sometimes in family law matters, the courts have to decide the ownership of the family home. In *C.F. v. C.F.* (2002) the applicant wife claimed ownership of the family home. Her husband had paid her father £100,000 for the property, but it had been registered in the wife's name. The husband said he ran his practice from the home. He claimed that he was the beneficial owner and sought a transfer order giving him legal title.

Mr Justice O'Sullivan held that, in the absence of any explicit agreement, the family home should be shared equally between them. He said the balance of fairness required him to make a property adjustment order vesting the legal and beneficial title of the family home in the husband, subject to his payment to the wife of a lump sum representing her half share in the home.

Any spouse who is asked to sign a document waiving rights under the 1976 Act should make sure to consult an experienced family law solicitor beforehand.

Chapter Eleven

Pensions And Tax

Tax and pension rights may be a very significant part of the financial considerations in a judicial separation or divorce. Nowadays, pension rights may represent a family's second biggest asset, after the family home. Pensions can be a complicated area and expert advice is likely to be needed when spouses separate.

Spouses may not arrange a pension adjustment order between themselves. Only the court has the power to make such an order. However, with the assistance of the lawyers on both sides and possibly actuaries, the court will often make such an order by consent.

The actuarial or transfer value of pension benefits depends on the member's salary, the type of pension scheme (public service or private sector), the amount of benefits and years of service in the scheme up to the date of the divorce. In many cases, the value of a pension in transfer terms may be greater than the value of the family home.

Pension rights and entitlements may involve:

- A pension at retirement age (or earlier if in ill health.)

- A spouse's pension on the death of the scheme member (before or after retirement.)

- A tax-free lump sum at retirement of up to one-and-a-half times final salary (depending on the length of service in the pension scheme).

- Contingent (life assurance) benefits, commonly of two to four times salary or more.

- An income for dependent children aged under 18 (or up to 23 if in full-time education).

The court is not required to make a pension adjustment order. It must first consider whether adequate or reasonable financial provision exists (or can be made) for the dependent spouse by using any other order.

Many employees are members of an occupational pension plan and their pension rights are generally regarded as "deferred pay." Equal pay legislation means many working women have also accumulated their own pension rights. There are generally two main types of pension scheme: defined *benefit* and defined *contribution*.

In a defined benefit scheme, retirement benefits are based on an individual's final pay and service with the employer. Benefits generally accrue at a set "pension fraction", such as 1/60th of pay for each year of service. This means a worker can predict in advance what percentage of his final pay will be received as a pension.

A defined contribution scheme usually works more like a conventional savings plan. The employee and employer both contribute to a special fund, which increases (or decreases) over the period leading to retirement, depending on whether the pensions investments go up or down. The eventual value of these benefits is unpredictable, as it will be influenced by the amount of contributions as well as the performance of the chosen investment.

Under the Pensions Act, employers must give employees a booklet containing details about pension rights and benefits, including whether the scheme is defined benefit or defined contribution.

Many employees also make additional voluntary contributions (AVC), which generally operate on the defined contribution basis.

People who are self employed (or not covered by an employer's occupational scheme) can take out "personal pensions" (or, more accurately, retirement annuity contracts) with insurance companies. These work on the principle of a defined contribution, with tax relief allowed up to a set total of contributions in each tax year.

Individuals working in family businesses may be members of either occupational or personal pension schemes, depending on the source of their earnings.

Pension schemes are run by trustees whose responsibilities are set out in the scheme's trust deed and rules, together with general trust law and the requirements of the Pensions Act 1990. A spouse or dependant may also be a potential beneficiary of the pension scheme and also has a right to information under the Pensions Act.

Employees should consult the trustees or scheme administrator to obtain details of their pension rights, although other experts – such as actuaries and consultants – may also be involved.

Benefits payable under different pension schemes will vary, but generally consist of:

- a retirement pension payable to the member;

- a pension payable to the member's spouse if the member dies *after* retirement;

- cash and a pension payable to the member's spouse (or dependants) if the member dies *before* retirement.

Middle-income workers are likely to have built up a reasonable level of pension rights by the time they're middle-aged. In the case of the self-employed or those working in family businesses, much of their personal wealth may still be secured in the business rather than through a pension plan, so pensions may not be such an important issue.

Until 1995, the courts could not divide up pensions as a specific asset on separation, although couples could make their own arrangements as part of an overall maintenance agreement. But the Family Law Act set out rules to deal with pension rights on judicial separation. The Divorce Act also gives the courts power to divide pension assets in the same way as other financial assets.

Pensions may only become a contentious issue if agreement can't be reached on splitting other assets, such as the home and any other property or financial holdings.

All pension rights may be taken into account on divorce or separation – including those accumulated before the marriage.

The court can order that part of the pension rights be paid to the spouse or to dependent children. If the spouse has already died, payment can be made to the estate of the deceased spouse.

The court can make orders about the pension benefits of either spouse. Generally a pension will be split at the time of a divorce, but either spouse can apply to the court for a pension adjustment order at any time during the lifetime of the pension scheme member. The application may also be made by a person acting on behalf of any dependent members of the family. The court may:

- transfer pension rights from one spouse to the other (a "clean break" approach), or

- set aside benefits due to be paid at a future date ("earmark assets").

Pension adjustment orders may be made against self-employed people and those in non-pensionable employment, as well as against members of occupational pension schemes.

Example 1

Mike, a self employed man, takes out a pension contract at 25. At 30, he marries Catherine. Ten years later, they separate. The court awards Catherine 50% of the pension. Mike's total contributions come to €20,000. The value of the fund is now €28,000. Catherine therefore receives a benefit worth €14,000.

Example 2

Brendan joined his employer's pension scheme when he was 20. He married Vera ten years later but they separated when he was 40. The court awards Vera 50% of the pension that accrued during their married life. Under the company scheme, Vera gets 1/60th of his salary for each year of service up to age 60. Vera's benefit when Brendan retires will be one twelfth of his salary (50% x 10/60 x final salary). At normal retirement age, Brendan will be entitled to 40/60 (or two thirds) of his final salary, less Vera's share, leaving Brendan with a pension of seven-twelfths of his final salary.

Where pension assets are split at the time of divorce under the "clean break" approach, part of the pension rights may be transferred to:

- the spouse's own pension arrangements (if a member of an occupational scheme) or

- an insurance company bond in the name of the receiving spouse.

Specialist advice will be required to work out the value of the amounts to be transferred, to represent the present day value of future entitlements.

As well as a retirement pension, the court can also order the pension scheme member to provide for a lump sum to be paid to the former spouse if the member dies before retirement. This benefit would cease if the receiving spouse remarried or died before the pension scheme member.

If a worker leaves his pensionable employment, the court will decide how much is due to the former spouse. The benefits can be kept in the pension scheme and paid later, or may be transferred to the spouse's scheme or an insurance bond. If a spouse leaves a pension scheme, the trustees must notify the other spouse and the court.

If a former spouse dies, the accumulated benefits (as decided by the court) must be paid to the estate within three months of the date of death. Depending on the arrangements made about death-in-service benefits, the lump sum and accumulated pension benefits may become payable to the former spouse at this stage.

If the former spouse has agreed to postpone a split of pension assets until retirement, the benefits are payable at that stage. In effect, both the member and the former spouse would become pensioners of the scheme. But if a dependent spouse remarries, any pension rights awarded by the court are forfeited to the original pension holder.

In order to assess the situation regarding a pension, the scheme member should provide his solicitor with a letter of authority addressed to the trustees authorising them to release information about the scheme and entitlements.

LETTER OF AUTHORITY

To whom it may concern

I _____ am a member of the _____ pension scheme. I hereby request and authorise the scheme trustees to provide such information about the scheme and my entitlements as may be requested by _____ solicitors.

Signed: _____

Date: _____

A change in marital status will also affect a person's tax position. Married couples living *together* may choose to be assessed for income tax by:

• single assessment,

• joint assessment, or

• separate assessment.

Spouses are not regarded as living together if they are separated by a formal agreement or court order, or if their separation is likely to be permanent.

The 1983 Finance Act deal with income tax assessment for separated spouses. Where a legally enforceable maintenance agreement existed before June 8, 1983, the payer deducts tax at the standard rate from maintenance payments. The recipient is taxed on the original gross amount, but receives a credit for the tax deducted at source.

If the maintenance agreement was made after June 8, 1983, the payer does not withhold income tax, but receives a deduction for payments made to a spouse. The recipient's payment is treated as income for tax purposes. Payments for dependent children are disregarded.

Parents who are not entitled to a married allowance may be entitled to a single parent allowance in respect of children who live with them for all or part of the year. Child allowance is payable for disabled children. Mortgage relief is limited to the single person's mortgage allowance, but may be allowable on loans for two properties.

Single treatment automatically applies when spouses separate unless they both request in writing to be assessed as if they were still living together. This does not apply to divorced couples or in the case of civil nullity. Both parties must be resident in the state and one spouse must be making payments under a maintenance agreement.

Spouses who are separately assessed submit their own individual tax returns and are entitled to their own personal allowances but pay tax only on their own income. Any unused personal allowances can be transferred to the other spouse.

Any maintenance payments are not taken into consideration (as there would be no such payments between a married couple), and the couple are taxed on a separate assessment basis.

If a person remarries, the Revenue Commissioners will recognise the new marriage, even if it is not recognised under the Domicile and Recognition of Foreign Divorces Act.

Different capital gains tax rules apply for separated couples in relation to their principal private residence, property transfers, share interaction, remarriage and death. The position of separated couples may also change with regard to capital acquisitions tax and stamp duty.

Where appropriate, spouses intending to separate or divorce should ask their solicitors to refer them to an experienced tax accountant.

Chapter Twelve

Wills

Marriage – or remarriage – revokes any previous will (unless the will was made in contemplation of that marriage), so people who change their marital status should also change their wills.

The 1965 Succession Act which lays down the requirements for a valid will, says that a spouse and children have a right to a certain share in the property of a deceased parent or spouse, whether a will was made or not.

Where a person dies leaving a spouse and no children, the spouse has a right to half the estate – whatever the will might say. If there are children of the marriage, the spouse has a right to one third of the estate.

The so-called "legal right" may be renounced in writing by a spouse at any time, but the courts would need to be quite sure that a spouse had received proper legal advice before giving up the right, and had not been subjected to any pressure.

In the case of *O'Dwyer v. Keegan* in 1997, a testator had died leaving £2.4 million. His wife, who was in a coma at the time, died 12 hours later, leaving £370,000. The husband had not provided for his wife in his will. The couple had no children and the wife had not renounced her legal right.

The High Court ruled that the "legal right" was merely a right, which the wife could have exercised if she wished. On appeal, the Supreme Court overruled that decision and said the "legal right" was automatically exercised when one spouse died.

The "legal right" has priority over any other bequests,

but may be extinguished by the court following a judicial separation and disappears after a divorce.

A spouse may try to evade the provisions of the statute by giving away all his property, but if he dies within three years of such dispositions, the gifts are void if they were made for that purpose. Of course, it might not always be possible for the other spouse to recover such void "gifts."

The law of probate, relating to wills, is largely contained in the 1965 Succession Act and Orders 79 and 80 of the Rules of the Superior Court. Most wills are "proved" simply by application to the Probate Office, without any reference to court. Sometimes there is a necessity for what is called a solemn form of proof, which requires a full court hearing and is binding on everyone involved.

For a will to be valid, the person making the will (known in legal terms as the testator – or testatrix if female) must be 18 years old or over (or have been married). He must also be acting of his own free will and be of "sound mind, memory and understanding." (A person who is entitled to appoint a guardian of a child may do so by will, even if he is under 18 and single.)

In the 19th century, Chief Justice Cockburn said a testator must:

1. understand that he is making a will, though he need not understand its precise legal effect,

2. know the nature and extent of his property (for example, he must not bequeath property which he had already given away), and

3. be able to recall the people who might be expected to benefit from his bounty (or to call to mind those who might have a claim against, or expect to benefit from, his estate).

A will may be challenged on the basis that the testator did

not have "testamentary capacity", that is the mental ability to make a valid will, though testamentary capacity may be proved by an affidavit from a doctor or solicitor who was present when the will was made, stating that the testator was of sound mind.

In the last resort, testamentary capacity is a matter for the courts, as the Supreme Court insisted in the 1987 case of *Glynn v. Glynn*. In that case, the testator's sister challenged his testamentary capacity after he left the balance of his estate to a cousin. He had already instructed a parish priest to draw up his will for him, but two months later he suffered a stroke that left him dumb. When the will was read back to him in hospital, he was only able to nod or shake his head. He marked an "X" at the end of the will.

A doctor testified that the deceased did not have testamentary capacity at the time, but the priest said he did. The High Court declared the will valid and the Supreme Court upheld that decision on appeal.

In *Blackall v. Blackall* (1996), a 99-year-old woman had made a will leaving her property equally between her four children. When her solicitor read the will over to her, the testatrix commented: "I think that's fair, one of them is a bit fiery". The judge said he was satisfied that was the comment of someone who knew what had been read to her, and that the testatrix did have testamentary capacity.

A blind person can make a will, but the Probate Office will require an affidavit from one of the witnesses, confirming that, if the testator had not been blind, he could have seen them sign. A blind person cannot be a witness as he is unable to see the testator sign.

Neither a witness *nor his spouse* may benefit under a will, except where:

- the legacy is a legal or moral duty, such as a debt,

- the benefit is given to a named beneficiary but in trust for someone else,

- the beneficiary and the witness married after the will, or
- the legacy is bequeathed in an additional clause to which the witness to the will is not a witness.

Even a clause agreeing a fee for drawing up or executing the will is void if the solicitor or a member of his firm (or their spouses) act as a witness. An executor who acts as a witness will lose any benefit.

A person who signs a will merely to show that he agrees with its contents, may benefit (although the will should indicate that he is not a witness).

A valid will must be in writing (oral wills for sailors or soldiers on military service are no longer permitted), and must be signed (or marked) at the end by the testator (or by someone in his presence and by his direction). The signature must be written or acknowledged before two witnesses, both present at the same time and the witnesses must sign in the presence of the testator.

A witness may be an executor of the will, or even a child – although this may cause problems if he is required to swear an affidavit while he is still a minor. The incompetence of a witness does not invalidate a will.

"Signature" can include the initials of the testator or, in the case of an illiterate or severely disabled person, a mark. In *Glynn v. Glynn* (1987), an X was accepted as a signature. In the 1960 case of *Cook*, the court proved a will signed simply "Your loving mother". In the case of a feeble signature or a mark, the Probate Office will require an affidavit from the witnesses, confirming that the will was read over by (or to) the deceased before execution and that he was of sound mind, memory and understanding.

A will is not necessarily invalidated simply because the signature does not immediately follow the last word or is after the witnesses' signatures, but any writing after the testator's signature is normally excluded as an unexecuted codicil. (A codicil is an addition to a will, which changes the original document.) The court decided in the 1974 case of *Beadle* that a document was not a will where the testatrix signed at the top of the page.

A will that does not comply with all these provisions will be valid if it complies with the law:

(1) of the place where the testator made it,

(2) of the testator's nationality (either when he made the will or at his death),

(3) of the place where the testator was domiciled or habitually resident when he made the will or died,

(4) of the place where immovable property is situated, or

(5) when a will is made on a ship or plane, where it had its most real connection.

A will should contain:

(1) the testator's name and address,

(2) a revocation clause,

(3) a clause appointing executors (preferably, but not necessarily, two or more),

(4) details of general and specific legacies (gifts of money or goods),

(5) details of devises (gifts of real property),

(6) a residuary clause, disposing of the remainder of the estate,

(7) the date,

(8) the testator's signature,

(9) the attestation clause or *testimonium,* and

(10) the witnesses' signatures.

The revocation clause must revoke all other codicils and earlier testamentary dispositions, as well as former wills. The executors, who should be likely to outlive the testator, should be clearly identified. "I appoint AB and CD as my executors" or "I appoint AB as my executor or, if he dies before me, I appoint CD in his place" are acceptable, but "I appoint AB or CD as my executor" would be void for uncertainty.

If the will has no residuary clause, any property not specifically mentioned would pass according to the rules of intestacy in the Succession Act. Also, if for any reason any of the other specific gifts should fail (for example, under the doctrine of lapse), the property involved would fall into the residue.

A will may contain only an executor clause and a residue clause, and still be valid if it expresses the wishes of the testator. If the executors have died or cannot (or will not) act, the person entitled to the residue can administer the estate.

The lack of a date on a will does not necessarily invalidate it, but the Probate Office will require an affidavit from one of the witnesses confirming that the document was executed before the testator died.

The *testimonium* might read: "Signed by the testator as and for his last will and testament in the presence of us, both present at the same time, and signed by us in the presence of the testator." The witnesses normally sign under this clause, but the will is not invalid if they sign elsewhere on the document. If the will does not contain a *testimonium*, the Probate Office will require an affidavit from one of the witnesses.

Wills "speak from death," and are interpreted as if they had been executed immediately before the death of the testator, unless the will itself specifies otherwise. If any children of the testator die before him, property bequeathed to them will automatically pass to their children.

If the will is in a foreign language, a translation may be admitted to proof. Any obliteration, insertion or alteration in a will after its execution is invalid unless:

- the testator and witnesses sign near the alteration,
- the changes are proved to have been in the will before its execution,
- the alterations are mentioned in the recital clause, or
- there is a properly-executed codicil or memorandum referring to the alterations.

If the will refers to any documents, which existed when the will was executed, they should be produced. If a will is written in pencil, a copy in red ink must be produced for the Probate Office. An official copy of any will or grant of administration may be obtained from the Probate Office or district probate registry.

A spouse who has deserted or committed a serious offence against the testator or against the testator's children loses any right to a share in the estate.

The court applied this rule in the 1992 case of *Martin Glynn* where the executor of a will murdered the testator's sister to obtain the family farm. The court held that the executor should not be granted probate.

A husband and wife's mutual rights to succeed to each other's estates may also be extinguished by the court at any time on or after a decree of judicial separation, under the 1995 Family Law Act. (Succession rights are automatically extinguished after a divorce, as the couple are no longer man and wife. Where a marriage is void, the partners are not spouses and these provisions also do not apply.)

A will may only be revoked by:

(1) a subsequent marriage – unless the will is made in contemplation of that marriage,

(2) a later will or codicil which expressly revokes all earlier testamentary dispositions,

(3) declaring in writing the intention to revoke the will, and executing the document in the same way as a will, or

(4) burning, tearing or destruction by the testator (or in his presence and at his direction), with the simultaneous intention of revocation.

If a testator writes to the person who holds the will, asking him to destroy it, that would revoke the will, whether or not it was actually destroyed. If no other will is executed, this would result in an intestacy.

Revocation of a will does not revive any earlier will; that may only be done by re-execution or a properly-executed codicil. However, there may be an implied revocation of an earlier will if a later will is clearly inconsistent with it – for example if the testator disposes of all his assets in the later will.

When a person dies, his estate is administered by a personal representative who can be either an executor (nominated in a will or codicil) or an administrator (where there is no will).

A personal representative holds the whole estate (real and personal) as trustee for anyone entitled to the property by law. Where someone dies without leaving a will (or executor), his estate vests in the President of the High Court until the Probate Office grants administration.

Applications for a grant of probate or letters of administration may be made in person or though a solicitor 14 days or more after the death of the deceased.

There are three types of primary grant of representation. A grant of probate only applies to the executors named in the will and simply confirms their authority. An executor does not have to act and is entitled to renounce his rights to administer the estate as long as he has not "intermeddled" in the estate – such as instructing a solicitor to prove the will.

A grant of administration with the will annexed is made where there is a valid will but the testator did not name an executor, or where the executor refuses to act.

A grant of administration intestate is made where there is no valid will and the deceased died wholly intestate. The Succession Act says that, if an intestate leaves a spouse and no children, the spouse takes the whole estate. If there are children, the spouse takes two thirds and the children share the remainder. If both spouses are dead, the children share the estate. If there is no surviving spouse and no issue, the estate goes to his parents or is divided according to sections 68-73 of the Act.

Most non-contentious problems with wills are dealt with by the Probate Office, but only the court may deal with lost or mislaid wills or disputes between rival applicants.

If a will has been lost, advertisements should be placed in appropriate newspapers and the *Law Society Gazette* to try and find it. The Probate Office will not accept a copy will, in case the original was revoked by destruction. An application must be made to court if the will is not found. At least one of the witnesses must swear that the will was properly executed and the solicitor who made the copy will must swear that it is authentic.

In the case of *Flood v. Flood* (1999), the executor had borrowed money from the testator and refused to repay it. The judge said the court could remove an executor in the case of "serious misconduct and/or serious special circumstances".

Anyone who wishes to challenge the terms of a will should lodge a warning notice or *caveat* in the Probate Office. The *caveat* should say:

> "Let nothing be done in the estate of (*name*) who died on (*date*) at (*address*) unknown to me (*name*) of (*address*), having interest."

The *caveat* remains in force for six months and may be renewed.

Anyone wishing to prove the will must issue a "*warning to caveat*" to the caveator, requiring him to enter an appearance in the Probate Office within six days to state his interest in the estate. A will may only be challenged by someone who would be entitled to benefit if it was struck down. A caveator may, for instance, have been a beneficiary in an earlier will or, if the caveator is the testator's next-of-kin, it might be in his interests to create an intestacy.

The caveator has to establish the nature of any problem with the will. There is a presumption that wills are duly executed and that the testator had testamentary capacity, so if the will appears valid, it is presumed to be so. These proceedings put the will beyond any subsequent challenge.

If the terms of a will are clear, the court will not allow extrinsic evidence about its construction. In the case of *O'Connell v. Bank of Ireland* (1998), a widow told several people that she had left her house and contents to the plaintiffs. But the will only mentioned the contents, not the house. The judge said he was quite satisfied that the testatrix had intended to leave her house to the plaintiffs, but he could only construe the will in accordance with its terms. The decision was upheld by the Supreme Court.

If the will is unclear, extrinsic evidence may be allowed to show the intention of the testator. In the case of *Lindsay v. Tomlinson* (1996), the testatrix left £25,000 to a non-existent charity, the "National Society for the Prevention of Cruelty to Animals (Dogs and Cats Home), 1 Grand Canal Quay in the city of Dublin." To confuse matters further, the Dublin Society for the Prevention of Cruelty to Animals and the Irish Society for the Prevention of Cruelty to Animals had formerly shared premises at 1 Grand Canal Quay.

The judge allowed evidence that the testatrix was a dog-lover, that she subscribed annually to the Dublin Society and that the Dublin Society operated the "Dogs and Cats Home" when it was situated at Grand Canal Quay. On the balance of probabilities, the judge said the scales came down in favour of the Dublin Society.

If the testator died wholly or partly testate, any of his children may bring an application under section 117 of the Succession Act claiming that he failed in the moral duty to make proper provision for his children. This action may be brought by a child of any age, whether adopted or not, whether born inside or outside the marriage and whether dependent or not.

In 1998, in the case of *E.B. v. S.S.*, the judge said: "Since the legislature, no doubt for good reasons, declined to impose any age ceiling which would preclude middle-aged or even elderly offspring from obtaining relief, the courts must give effect to the provision, irrespective of the age which the child has attained."

The court will consider the claim from the point of view of a "prudent and just parent," taking into account any payments made during the testator's lifetime and the situation of any other children, but disregarding the testator's attitude to the applicant.

In the case of *G.M.* (1972), the judge said the court would consider:

(1) the amount left to the surviving spouse (or the value of the legal right),

(2) the number of the testator's children,

(3) the ages and positions in life of the children at the testator's death,

(4) the means of the testator,

(5) the age of the applicant,

(6) the financial position and prospects of the applicant and

(7) any other provision already made by the testator for the applicant.

The court ruled in the case of *McDonald v. Norris* (1999) that it could also take into account a plaintiff's behaviour towards his parent.

In *Browne v. Sweeney* (1998), the plaintiff's mother bequeathed £5,000 to each of her grandchildren and divided the residue of her estate – worth about £1.3 million – between five charities. The plaintiff and his three siblings had each received about £275,000 five years before their mother's death. The plaintiff suffered from drink and drug addiction and had wasted the money. The judge said that, in the circumstances, the testatrix had discharged her moral duty and he dismissed the claim.

A child who has been found guilty of an offence against the deceased (or against any spouse or child of the deceased) punishable by two years' imprisonment or more, may not make an application under section 117.

A section 117 application must be made within six months of the first taking out of representation of the estate. This limitation period cannot be extended by the court and applies whether or not it is raised as a defence.

The danger of making a series of wills was illustrated by the High Court case of *Felix Smyth v. John Halpin and Regina Stokes* (1996). Felix Smyth was brought up on a farm in Castletown, Co. Meath. In 1987, he decided to marry and asked his father to give him a site to build a house. His father replied: "This place is yours after your mother's day – what would you be doing with two places?"

The father made a number of wills. In the earliest, dated 1966, he bequeathed his house and farm to his wife, and on her death to Felix's brother, Ian. The father's next will, dated 1976, bequeathed the house and farm to his wife and, on her death, to Felix.

The next will, dated 1986, left the farm and house to his wife and thereafter to Felix, subject to the right of his daughters to choose a half-acre site each on which to build a house. The next will, dated 1991, bequeathed the farm to his wife and thereafter to the plaintiff without conditions. The house was bequeathed to Felix's mother for her life and thereafter to his sister Regina.

Under the last will, dated 1992, the father appointed John Halpin and another man as executors and bequeathed the lands to his wife for her life and thereafter to Felix absolutely. He also bequeathed the house to his wife for life and thereafter to Regina.

Felix only learned of the father's change of mind in relation to the house when the will was read out after the death. He asked the High Court to declare that he was entitled to the house after the death of his mother.

Mr Justice Geoghegan referred to the English case of *Inwards v. Baker* (1965) where a father had suggested to his son that he build on his land – which the son then did at his own expense. The Court of Appeal held that the son had an equitable right to remain in the house for the rest of his life, even though the father had left all his property to a lady with whom he had lived for some years.

The judge ruled that Felix had "clearly established that he falls within these (equitable) principles" and he directed that a deed be executed to vest the remainder interest in the house in Felix.

A legal guardian of a child may appoint a person in a will to be guardian of that child (known as a "testamentary guardian"). If the parents of a child are married to one another and one dies, the surviving spouse automatically assumes sole guardianship. If the parents are not married but have joint guardianship, it is particularly important that both should appoint a testamentary guardian in their wills.

Wills can be very straightforward where a couple intend leaving all their property to the other or in equal shares between their children. Separation, divorce or remarriage introduce all sorts of complications. Anyone who has already made a will – or, indeed, anyone who has not yet made a will – and intends to separate or remarry should take legal advice before drawing up a new will.

Chapter Thirteen

Legal Aid

The Legal Aid Board was established in 1979 to administer the scheme of civil legal aid and advice. The purpose of the Board is to make the advice of solicitors and barristers available to people who have little or no money. Costs of the scheme are met by Government grant which totalled €17.3 million in 2001.

Most legal aid services are provided by full-time legal aid solicitors at 30 Law Centres around the country. Since 1993, the Board has also used private solicitors for maintenance, custody and barring matters in the District Court. The services of barristers are also available, under a different scheme.

In 2001, just over 18,700 clients received legal services, a rise of 900 on the previous year. In June 2002, waiting periods varied up to seven months, so those in need of urgent advice may have to seek advice from a private family law solicitor.

The overwhelming majority of all civil legal aid cases are concerned with family law. In 2001, the Board provided legal aid in 1,469 District Court family law cases, with private practitioners used by the Legal Aid Board in a further 1,174 cases. In the Circuit Court, 2,257 cases were handled by Legal Aid Board solicitors or private solicitors on their behalf.

The number of legal aid certificates granted in judicial separation cases rose to 820 in 2001, while divorce accounted for the biggest number of Circuit Court cases, at 991. Legal aid was also provided for 78 High Court cases.

The principles applicable to legal aid in family law cases

involving children were set out by the Supreme Court in the case of *M.F. v. Legal Aid Board* (1993).

In cases involving the custody, guardianship and welfare of a child of married parents, it is only necessary for the Legal Aid Board to conclude that there is a "reasonable likelihood" that the judge will take into account the applicant's point of view and submissions. The "benefit of the applicant" in the statute should be interpreted as meaning the applicant's interest in the welfare of a child. The same principles would apply to appeals or variations of orders relating to children.

Applicants for legal aid will be asked to fill in a form to assess their income. Anyone with a *disposable* income of less than €13,000 a year may be entitled to legal aid. The maximum allowances that may be set against income for the purpose of calculating eligibility are:

- Applicant's spouse €1,900

- Dependent child €1,100

- Child care €1,100

- Accommodation €4,900

- Income tax – full amount

- Social insurance – full amount

- *Ex gratia* payments €1,040

If the case goes to court, the Legal Aid Board will also take into account the value of the applicant's capital resources (such as his house, land, car or savings), and may also require payment of a capital contribution.

Examples of operation of means test

(1) Single parent with four children

Gross income €13,565 and lone parent allowance of €10,192 (total €23,757), less allowances of €11,173, comprising:

- 4 children €4,400

- Rent €3,840

- Childcare €1,040

- PRSI €746

- PAYE €1,147

Disposable income: €12,584. Contribution payable €1,106.

(2) Married person with two children and non-dependent spouse

Gross income €18,067 less allowances of €8,779 comprising:

- 2 children €2,200

- Mortgage €4,900

- PRSI €762

- PAYE €917

Disposable income: €9,288. Contribution payable €282.

(3) Single person with three children

Gross income €11,458 and lone parent allowance of €7,108 (total €18,566) less allowances of €10,400 comprising:

- 3 children €3,300

- Rent €4,900

- Childcare €2,200

Disposable income: €8,166. Contribution payable €35.

(4) Married person with one child and non-dependent spouse

Gross income €17,620 less allowances of €7,847 comprising:

- 1 child €1,100

- Mortgage €4,900

- PRSI €458

- PAYE €1,389

The minimum contribution – payable by a person whose disposable income does not exceed €8,300 a year – is €6 for legal *advice* and €35 for legal *aid*. The maximum contribution is €1,210.

One of the problems with legal aid can be the delay in waiting to see a solicitor. In *Kavanagh v. Legal Aid Board* (2001), a woman who had applied in September 1997 for legal aid in connection with a judicial separation complained that she had to wait nearly two years for her application to be granted.

The separation proceedings were eventually instituted in April 2000 and had been concluded by the time of her High Court application.

Elizabeth Kavanagh sought damages for the Board's failure to consider her application within a reasonable time, as required by the 1995 Legal Aid Act.

The judge said that the act required the Board to provide legal aid and advice "within the Board's resources." The Board said that meant, not just financial resources, but also the availability of personnel. The Board's limited resources had been stretched due to a number of factors, including the introduction of divorce.

Refusing the claim for damages, the judge said: "The words [of the act] simply mean that legal aid shall be provided within the Board's resources and I am fully satisfied ... that that is precisely what the Board did in this case. The Board had a method of dealing with cases in a certain order of priority and, within that scheme, the applicant was given equal treatment to all other applicants."

Those who cannot afford a solicitor may also be able to obtain help from the free legal advice centres. FLAC is a non-governmental organisation, which was set up in 1969 to campaign for the introduction of a comprehensive scheme of civil legal aid and advice.

Today, FLAC provides a general legal advice service through a network of part-time clinics in Dublin and Cork, staffed by volunteer barristers and solicitors. During office hours, the head office in Dublin also operates a telephone information and referral line.

Chapter Fourteen

Your Day in Court

For many people involved in marriage breakdown, the thought of going to court may fill them with apprehension. Perhaps that is why so many cases settle on the steps of the court. However, it's not quite as bad as it may seem.

In general, all family law matters are heard *in camera*, that is in private. The only people allowed in court – apart from the judge and the spouses – are the lawyers (possibly a barrister and solicitor on each side), the registrar, the judge's tipstaff and maybe a stenographer. Witnesses who may give evidence will leave court as soon as they have finished testifying.

Many of the preliminary matters in family law are dealt with in the District Court. Ireland is divided into 23 districts – 22 provincial districts and the Dublin Metropolitan District. The president of the District Court and his 50 judges sit at 200 venues around the country.

The District Court is a court of local jurisdiction, which means that cases are allocated to courts in the area where one of the parties lives or works.

The powers of the District Court and the amounts that it can award are limited by statute. The court deals with a range of family law matters, including applications for safety, protection and barring orders, maintenance orders (up to €500 a week for a spouse and €150 a week for each child), applications for custody, access and guardianship and declarations of paternity.

In the year ending July 31, 2000, the District Court dealt with 23,452 family law cases. Of those, 10,314 were heard in Dublin. More than half of the applications related to domestic violence.

When proceedings are instituted, the office starts a file and gives the case its own file number. That number is used throughout all the related proceedings and applications, and details are maintained on the file in the court office.

District Court staff also issue summonses, prepare the list of cases for court, issue arrest warrants, draw up court orders, collect and pay out certain maintenance orders and process documents for Circuit Court appeals.

The Circuit Court deals with a wide range of family law cases, including nullity, judicial separation, divorce, District Court appeals and applications to dispense with the three-month waiting period for a couple planning to marry.

In the context of divorces and judicial separation applications, the Circuit Court can also deal with many of the same matters as the District Court, including barring orders, child custody, guardianship and access, maintenance, financial orders (including lump sums, pensions and succession rights) and property orders.

In Dublin, the Circuit Family Court sits in new offices in Smithfield, not far from the Four Courts. Around the country, family law matters are generally heard in the family court on different days from other civil and criminal matters.

The High Court will generally deal with "big money" cases, and it also acts as a court of appeal from the Circuit Court. A case, which is appealed from the Circuit Court to the High Court, may not be further appealed in Ireland except on a point of law.

In *B. (N.) v. B. (M.)* (2002), the husband asked the Supreme Court to extend time for an appeal against a High Court order made on appeal from a Circuit Court order.

The wife had claimed a decree of divorce and property orders, but the husband argued that the couple's property rights had been disposed of in proceedings many years earlier. He said the application to the Circuit Court was an abuse of process.

The Supreme Court said the husband was aggrieved by the fact that there appeared to be no finality to his matrimonial problems but there was no doubt about the legal principles applicable: the Supreme Court had "no jurisdiction to hear an appeal from the High Court exercising its appellate jurisdiction in respect of decisions of the Circuit Court."

Parties in family law cases may have to endure several appearances in court, depending on the nature of the case. Sometimes there may be a series of interim applications relating to such matters as barring, maintenance, access or property, which arise urgently and have to be dealt with before the substantive hearing.

On other occasions, particularly where there is agreement between the parties or in the matter of consent divorces, there will only be one short court hearing.

It is usually better if a husband and wife can come to an agreement – even if neither obtains everything desired – rather than let a judge make a decision which both may find completely unsatisfactory. If a deal can be hammered out – preferably at an early stage – it can be "ruled" by the court and given the force of a court order.

If, despite the best efforts of everyone, agreement cannot be reached, a court hearing becomes inevitable.

Parties should normally arrive at court before 10am to meet their solicitor and barrister. The lawyers will explain the probable sequence of events and may indicate what matters are likely to be raised – though they may not coach witnesses.

At 10.30 am, there is normally a call-over of the day's list of cases, at which stage all the lawyers appear in court to inform the judges sitting that day either that their case has been settled, or that it requires an adjournment or is going ahead.

After the call-over, short matters (such as consent divorces and marriage exemptions) may be heard first to allow the parties in those matters to leave. For the rest of the cases on the list, it can be a very long wait, with no guarantee that all listed matters will be heard on the day.

Anyone appearing in court should dress soberly and appropriately. Once called into court, the applicant and respondent will sit at the back of the court while the lawyers sit at a table at the front. Normally, the barristers will face the judge, while the instructing solicitors will sit on the other side of the table with their backs to the judge, facing the barrister. In complicated cases or in the High Court, there may be two barristers, senior and junior counsel.

The case is opened by the barrister for the applicant who will outline the matter to the judge. The applicant's case is heard first and the applicant will be called to give sworn evidence in the witness box. The applicant's barrister may not "lead" by asking questions, which suggest a certain answer. If a barrister does ask leading questions, the respondent's barrister may interrupt and object.

At the end of the examination-in-chief, the respondent's barrister will cross-examine the witness. If new matters are raised in cross-examination, the applicant's barrister may briefly re-examine the witness at the end of the cross-examination. Finally, the judge will clarify any unclear matters and the applicant will then be given permission to leave the witness box.

All the witness's answers to questions should be directed in a loud, clear voice to the judge. In the Circuit Court and High Court, the judge is addressed as "My Lord," whether male or female. In the District Court, the judge is addressed as "Judge". If a question is unclear, the barrister should be asked to repeat or explain it.

Apart from the spouses, other witnesses may be called. Children may give evidence in certain circumstances. Other witnesses may include family members, doctors, psychologists, accountants, estate agents and gardaí.

Spouses should not interrupt the proceedings, even if they

disagree with the evidence being given. If something urgent should be drawn to counsel's attention, a note should be discreetly passed to the solicitor. It is not in a spouse's interest to interrupt the concentration of his lawyers unless the matter is really important.

Giving evidence can take hours – and some cases may take days. The courts sit from 11am to 1pm, then rise for lunch and sit again from 2pm to 4pm. If the court adjourns during a person's evidence, the legal team may not discuss the evidence with the witness during the break.

Sometimes settlement talks may resume in the middle of a case when one side begins to see sudden unanticipated strengths or weakness in the other side's case. A judge will always allow time for talks if requested to do so. Similarly, if one side decides that the talks are at an end, the judge is bound to resume the case.

If the matter is very complicated, the judge may reserve judgment, that is deliver a written judgment at a later date. Either side may appeal a judgment.

Appearing in court may be very stressful, but it's important to remember that the family law judges are very experienced and are used to courtroom nerves. They and the lawyers will do what they can to make the difficult occasion as straight-forward as possible.

Chapter Fifteen

Unmarried Couples

So called 'common law marriage' is not recognised in Ireland and unmarried couples cannot generally claim the benefit of marital legislation.

In *The State (Nicolaou) v. An Bord Uchtála* (1966), Henchy J said: "For the state to award equal constitutional protection to the family founded on marriage and the 'family' founded on an extramarital union would in effect be a disregard of the pledge which the state gives in Article 41 [of the Constitution] to guard with special care the institution of marriage."

If an unmarried couple split up – even if they have children – there is no obligation on either person to support the former partner.

This was decided in the High Court case of *Bernadette Ennis v. Colm Butterly* (1997). The couple were both married but separated. In 1985 they started to live together and bought a house in joint names. They agreed that when divorce was available in Ireland, they would seek a divorce from their current spouse and marry each other as soon as possible.

Ennis paid all the mortgage payments and household expenses, while Butterly gave her money for herself and her son. Butterly also paid his wife maintenance.

In 1993, Ennis learned that Butterly was occasionally living with his wife so she threw him out. Butterly begged her for forgiveness; he promised to marry her as soon as possible, gave her another engagement ring, asked her to live full-time at home, promised to pay all household outgoings, said she could have her own current account and access to his credit card account, said he would give her half of a £350,000 cheque, offered to make her a director and shareholder in his company and promised he would be faithful to her.

In return, she agreed to marry him as soon as they were both free, and in the meantime she would give up work and stay at home full-time.

But in 1994, Ennis learned that Butterly was having an affair with another woman, and she told him to leave home. Butterly said he would still honour his financial commitments to her, but he failed to do so. Ennis claimed damages for breach of contract, as well as negligent and fraudulent misrepresentation.

The court said that the breach of contract related to an agreement to marry and an agreement to live together as man and wife until they could marry each other, in return for which Ennis had given up her business and lived as a full-time homemaker.

But the court said that the Family Law Act 1981 abolished actions for breach of promise of marriage. In any case, Ennis and Butterly were each married to someone else. Even before the 1981 Act, their agreement to marry each other would have been unenforceable as a matter of public policy.

Butterly said the proceedings were, in effect, a claim for "palimony" based on the decision of the Supreme Court of California in *Marvin v. Marvin* (1976) which said: "The courts should enforce express contracts between non-marital partners, except to the extent that the contract is explicitly founded on the consideration of meretricious sexual services."

The High Court said it would not follow the US decision, but preferred the English case of *Windeler v. Whitehall* (1990), in which the judge said: "A husband has a legal obligation to support his wife, even if they are living apart. A man has no legal obligation to support his mistress, even if they are living together." Mr Justice Peter Kelly said:

"Given the special place of marriage and the family under the Irish Constitution, it appears to me that the public policy of this state ordains that non-marital cohabitation does not and cannot have the same constitutional status as marriage.

"To permit an express cohabitation contract to be enforced would give it a similar status in law to a marriage contract ... As a matter of public policy, such agreements cannot be enforced.

"Whether one calls it palimony or not, it is not capable of enforcement in this jurisdiction ... If it is not a palimony claim, it is clearly an attempt to enforce a contract, the consideration for which is wifely services being rendered on the part of a mistress. Such contracts were always regarded as illegal and unenforceable and remain so."

The position regarding the children of unmarried couples also differs markedly from that of married couples. The offspring of an unmarried couple are now called "non-marital children," rather than "illegitimate." They retain the same rights as marital children to the estates of both their parents – but unmarried fathers in Ireland have very limited rights to their children.

First of all, an unmarried father may need to prove that he is the father of the child concerned. Under the 1987 Status of Children Act, a court can order a blood test to determine the parentage of a child. (Conversely, the 1987 Act also allows a child to seek a declaration by the Circuit Court that a person is his mother or father – even if the parent is dead. This is likely to be of particular relevance in probate cases.)

Where a couple are not married, the Supreme Court has ruled that the father has no automatic right to be guardian to his children.

In *W. O'R. v. E.H. and the Adoption Board* (1996), the couple had been involved in a relationship from 1981 to 1992 and had two children. They lived together as a family for the last six years of their relationship and considered getting married.

But 11 months after the birth of their son, they separated permanently. The mother married another man in 1993 and she and her husband applied to the Adoption Board to adopt the two children.

The natural father applied to the District Court to be appointed guardian of the children but was refused, though he was granted access to his children. The Adoption Board said it would not make any adoption order until the access order had been removed.

An adoption order may not normally be made without the consent of the child's mother or guardian. Under the Adoption Act 1952, the mother or guardian of a child loses all parental rights and duties if an adoption order is made.

The natural father said he would oppose the adoption order if he were appointed guardian, though he did not intend to seek custody of the children.

Under the 1964 Guardianship of Infants Act, the mother of an illegitimate child is its guardian. Before 1987, the natural father only had a right to make an application for custody and access. He had no right to apply to be appointed guardian. Now, if both parents agree, they may swear a statutory declaration for the father to become a joint guardian (see page 256). If the mother does not agree to this, the father may apply to the court under the 1987 Status of Children Act to be made a guardian.

In *J.K. v. V.W.* (1990), the Supreme Court said the Act only gave the natural father the right to *apply* to be appointed guardian. It did not give him a right to *be* guardian, and did not mean his position was the same as that of a father married to the mother of the child.

Chief Justice Thomas Finlay said the rights of an unmarried father towards his child varied from a situation where the child was conceived as the result of casual intercourse (where the rights might be practically non-existent) to a child born in a situation with nearly all the characteristics of a constitutionally protected family (when the rights would be "very extensive indeed").

The Supreme Court said the basic issue for any judge was the welfare of the children, so he must consider all relevant factors, including the blood link and the relationship between the father and mother when the child was conceived – though these were subordinate to the paramount concern, which was the welfare of the children. It was up to the judge to decide what was best for the welfare of the children.

An unmarried father may be unable to prevent the adoption of his child by someone else, even when he is living with the child's mother. In *C.M. v. Delegación Provincial de Malaga and A.B. and C.D.* (1999), C.M. had been born in Spain in 1995 and had been adopted there by A.B. and C.D., through the agency of the Delegación Provincial.

C.'s mother, O.M., was an Irish citizen, resident and domiciled in Ireland, and was unmarried. C.'s father, P.H., was three years older and a barman. He was married with one child, but his marriage had broken down.

In 1995, after the mother went to Spain to work, she realised she was pregnant. P.H. joined her there and the baby girl was born in Malaga. The couple looked after the baby for about seven weeks, but found that too difficult and eventually gave her up for adoption.

OM then moved back to Ireland and set up house with P.H. In April 1996, she and P.H. went to the Spanish embassy in Dublin and asked to have C. returned to them. In September 1996, O.M. instructed Spanish lawyers to apply to the courts in Spain for the return of her child.

In 1998, the Malaga court refused the parents' application for access to C. and said that the adoption should be dealt with under Spanish law. The court also decided that both parents should be deprived of guardianship of their child, on the grounds that they had abandoned her. The parents appealed and applied to the Irish courts for an order requiring the return of C. under the Hague Convention and 1991 Child Abduction and Enforcement of Custody Orders Act.

The High Court accepted that, even when a child was not in Ireland, it still had power to declare that the removal from the state of a child who was an Irish citizen was wrongful – though it could only do this if the child's "habitual residence" was Ireland.

The court said a person, whether a child or an adult, must have been actually present in a country for at least some reasonable period of time before he or she could be habitually resident there. In this case, the child had never been to Ireland.

The judge said the Adoption Acts specifically permitted the adoption of a child of unmarried parents and said the father had no constitutional rights in regard to the child.

The position of the parents was a "sad one," said the judge, but if they wanted to pursue their claim for the return of the child, they would have to do so in the Spanish courts.

While pre-nuptial agreements are not legally binding for married couples, it is sensible for unmarried couples to arrange their affairs – particularly in relation to property – by prior written agreement. Both must have independent legal advice if these agreements are subsequently to withstand the scrutiny of a court.

Chapter Sixteen

Remarriage in Church

Most people in Ireland marry in church, yet not everyone distinguishes between the two distinct components to the marriage: the religious element and the civil element.

The civil element is a straightforward contract between the parties to remain mutually faithful and support one another until death or the breakdown of the contract.

The understanding of the religious element of marriage depends on the spouses' philosophical and doctrinal beliefs.

The most recent census figures indicate that 92% of the population of the Republic claim to be Catholics, less than 3% are members of the Church of Ireland and under half of one per cent are Presbyterians. The remaining 5% comprise members of other Christian and non-Christian religions, together with non-believers.

The overwhelming majority of church marriages in the Republic of Ireland are Catholic Church marriages. And, as far as Catholic teaching is concerned, marriage is one of the seven sacraments and is for life. Validly married Catholics may not remarry in a Catholic church while the other spouse is still alive.

For practising Catholics who wish to end their marriage and remarry in church, the only solution that might be available is an ecclesiastical decree of nullity.

While other Christian Churches all accept the ideal of marriage as a union in which the couple swear lifelong fidelity, only the Catholic Church refuses to accept the remarriage of divorced people in church – unless the "marriage" has first been annulled by the Church.

Anglicans

The four Anglican churches in these islands have no uniform policy on the remarriage of divorced people. The Church of England officially permits the religious remarriage of divorced people in "exceptional circumstances". As it is the established Church of the State, its clergymen are also civil registrars, and occasionally use that authority to remarry divorced people in church.

The Scottish Episcopal Church decided in 1981 to allow the remarriage of divorced people in church, at the discretion of the local bishop. The Anglican Church in Wales allows the practice at the discretion of the vicar except in the case of serial remarriage, where the bishop should be consulted.

The Church of Ireland – which has 90,000 members in the Republic – regularised the procedure for the remarriage of divorcees in 1996.

A cleric must first ask the opinion of the local bishop. Once the bishop has given an opinion, the cleric decides whether he or she is prepared to officiace at the marriage. If the cleric refuses to officiate, the bishop will appoint someone who will do so.

If the remarriage goes ahead, the cleric may conduct a private penitential service with the couple in preparation for remarriage in church.

Presbyterians and Methodists

The Presbyterian and Methodist Churches, while subscribing to the principle of lifelong marriage, accept that relationships do break down and both permit the remarriage of divorced people in church.

Baptists

Baptists are congregationalists, so do not have an overall Church teaching on the remarriage of divorced persons. Many

Baptists would allow divorce on the Biblical grounds of unfaithfulness or desertion. It is a matter for the members and leaders of each local church to decide on the facts of the specific case, whether a particular Baptist should be allowed to remarry in church.

Greek Orthodox

Couples who marry in Dublin's Greek Orthodox Church and subsequently divorce may remarry in church after obtaining an ecclesiastical divorce from the Church authorities. This is *not* the same as an ecclesiastical decree of nullity. The Church authorities accept the validity of the first marriage but may grant a Church divorce for adultery or other serious matters. The second church marriage is also regarded as a sacrament, but has something of a penitential character.

Muslims

There are now more than 12,000 Muslims in Ireland, with their own purpose-built mosque in Clonskeagh and smaller mosques in Cork, Galway, Limerick and Ballyhaunis, Co Mayo. Islam permits polygamy – up to four wives per husband. The official position of Islam in relation to divorce is that it is undesirable except as a last resort. When divorce does occur, however, it is effected simply by the husband telling his wife three times "I divorce you".

There is no difficulty with remarriage for divorced Muslims, but their mosque is not a recognised building for marriages because of the conflict between Islamic law and Irish law. If Moslems wish to have their marriage recognised by the State, they have to be married by a civil registrar.

Catholics

The Catholic Church does not permit the remarriage of anyone who has gone through a valid Catholic marriage ceremony and whose spouse is still alive – whether divorced or not. The only way a Catholic may marry in church in such circumstances is if the Church is prepared to declare the original marriage null and void.

A Catholic Church nullity decree (or "ecclesiastical nullity") may only be obtained if there was a serious problem from the start of the marriage. Such problems would include lack of full consent, impotence, a forbidden degree of relationship between the spouses (such as a godparent marrying an unrelated godchild before1983) or where one or both the parties is unbaptised.

The decree affects *only* the religious element of the marriage. Catholics who have received a Church nullity, but who have not been divorced or been granted a State nullity, may *not* remarry in a register office. Anyone who did so would be committing the crime of bigamy.

Catholics who have been granted an ecclesiastical decree of nullity (without a civil decree or divorce) may marry in church without the need for a dissolution of a pre-existing valid civil marriage, but the marriage is valid *only* in the eyes of the Catholic Church. The State will not recognise the second marriage as valid.

In the case of *People v. Ballins* (1964), Mrs Christina Ballins had gone through a civil marriage with William Ballins in a register office in Cornwall in 1954. They had one daughter. Soon afterwards, she returned to Ireland where she met and lived with John Kenny for 12 months. She tried to divorce her husband but he said he would only agree if he could have custody of the daughter. She refused and went through a Catholic Church wedding to Mr Kenny in 1960. (The Catholic Church does not recognise the validity of a register office wedding where either partner is a Catholic.)

The judge said there was a serious conflict between the civil law and canon law. Normally he would impose an 18-month prison sentence for bigamy, but in this case, he bound her over in the sum of £50 to keep the peace for two years.

It must be established with moral certainty that there are grounds for nullity because of a fundamental defect present at the time of the marriage

In Ireland, the increase in the number of nullity decrees granted by the Catholic Church has been dramatic. In 1981, 67 couples were granted ecclesiastical decrees of nullity in the 32 counties – although, in 48 cases, one of the partners was refused permission to remarry. In 1990, 216 couples were granted Church nullities and by 1996, that figure had risen to 347.

The introduction of divorce – and, presumably, the resulting ability to remarry – led to a surge in Church nullity applications in 1996/7, with 582 Church annulments granted in 1997.

The figures have now levelled off, with 477 decrees granted in 2000 – all of them on the basis of invalid consent. Seven cases were sent to Rome with a recommendation for a dispensation from a ratified but unconsummated marriage. There was just one application for a declaration of the presumed death of a spouse. Just over 900 petitions were outstanding at the end of 2000.

Only a minority of the applications continue beyond the initial stage. About 40% are found to have no apparent basis, while another one third are withdrawn by the applicants. Of those that continue to a full hearing, about 90 % are granted.

A Church nullity decree – despite some popular misconceptions – is not only available to the rich. While the lawyers' bill in a *civil* nullity action (without legal aid) could, in some cases, run to many thousands of euros, a Church nullity will cost only a fraction of that.

Anyone applying for a Church nullity will be asked to make an initial contribution of €50. If the case is accepted, the maximum fee would be around €700, plus €125 for a psychological assessment – though this may be waived in cases of genuine hardship.

If the Tribunal eventually decides that the case merits further investigation, the applicant will be asked to pay a fee (in instalments, if necessary) towards the costs of the proceedings. But the Tribunal tells applicants:

> "If you are genuinely unable to pay all, or any, part of the costs, the Church will gladly come to your aid in meeting whatever deficit is involved."

In practice, only a minority pay the full fee. Over a third of petitioners pay nothing, while most of the others pay between €120 and €320.

If the case is accepted for hearing, both spouses will be invited for an interview. Each is required to give a statement on oath and may be requested to undergo psychological assessment. If one party refuses to co-operate, the tribunal may decide the case on the evidence of the other spouse alone. The tribunal hearing is in private; not even the spouses are allowed to be present. The representatives of each spouse put the arguments to a judge, who decides the matter.

In about 75-80% of cases where a Church nullity decree is granted, one or both of the parties are not permitted to remarry because the Church considers that the defect which caused the nullity (such as a psychological problem) still exists and would put in danger any future marriage. The veto may be lifted by the local bishop only if he is satisfied, after an investigation, that the person is fit for marriage in all essential respects.

Before a decree is granted, the case must be judged by two independent tribunals. In Ireland they are a regional tribunal and the National Appeals Tribunal. Both tribunals must establish with moral certainty (probability is not enough) that nullity exists because of a fundamental defect of capacity or consent at the time of the marriage. As in a civil nullity application, there is a presumption of validity and it is up to the applicant to prove otherwise.

The process of obtaining a Church nullity decree in Ireland may take four years or more from start to finish. The Code of Canon Law, which governs Church regulations on marriage on nullity, is available online at www.intratext.com/x/eng0017.htm

Chapter Seventeen

Questions and Answers

These are just a few of the questions emailed to Kieron Wood by the tens of thousands of visitors to his website at http://welcome.to/barrister. Details have been altered where necessary to protect the privacy of the inquirer.

Q. *I have come to Ireland and found the love of my life and we want to get married. The lady in question had a Catholic Church annulment of her marriage. Does that mean we can marry or does she have to get a divorce also?*

A. A Church nullity has NO effect on the status of a civil marriage. It relates only to the religious element of the marriage and simply means that a person may remarry in a Catholic Church. Your girlfriend will need to get a divorce to marry you.

Q. *Congratulations on your excellent website. You say: "You can't get an Irish divorce unless at least one spouse is domiciled in the Republic or has lived in the country for a year before bringing proceedings." Does this mean you must live in Ireland for a year immediately before bringing proceedings or at any time during one's life?*

A. A person must have lived in Ireland for at least one year at the date of institution of divorce proceedings.

Q. *Could you please give me guidelines for an Irish person living in America seeking a divorce. My spouse still lives in*

Ireland with our three children.

A. The Irish courts may grant a divorce where either spouse was domiciled in the state on the date of institution of proceedings or where either spouse had been ordinarily resident in the state for one year, ending on the date of the institution of proceedings. You also must have been separated for four out of the past five years.

Q. *Wondering if you can direct me to information regarding marriage of Irish citizens abroad who are marrying citizens of another country. I am not Irish and I am divorced and we are having a hard time with getting a* certificat de coûtume. *Any help would be appreciated.*

A. A marriage abroad is subject to local law. Whether or not you are a foreigner or divorced is a matter for local law, not for Irish law. If you were divorced in Ireland, you can obtain a copy of the decree from the family court office. You can obtain further information from the Registrar of Marriages in Dublin.

Q. *What proof do we need to provide to the court that we have been separated for four years? During that period, we moved out and back more than once. Do both parties have to agree on the length of the separation?*

A. As long as you were separated for four of the five years before applying for a divorce, that will satisfy the statute. It has nothing to do with the agreement of the parties; it is a matter of fact. If you both agree on the dates, the court is likely accept them, unless it has other evidence to the contrary. Proof of separate addresses (such as utility bills) would also be helpful. Living apart does not necessarily imply living in separate houses, but it does mean that there was no marital relationship.

Q. *Can you please tell me how long it takes to obtain a divorce under Irish law? I am resident in Holland, as is my wife.*

A. You can't seek an Irish divorce unless at least one of you is domiciled in the Republic of Ireland or has lived in the country for a year before bringing proceedings.

Q. *I was married in England but my four children and I are resident in Ireland. My husband is seeking a divorce from me as we have been separated for over two years. He lives and works in England. Can I be represented by a solicitor in Ireland or do I have to use a solicitor based in England?*

A. If your husband has already initiated divorce proceedings in England, it would be usual to use a solicitor practising in England, although, under EU law, any practising lawyer in one state can practise in all other EU states, subject to certain limitations. If he has not yet initiated proceedings, you should consider issuing proceedings in Ireland.

Q. *Is there a way to go about getting a legal separation without going through the courts? Are there any forms for this?*

A. You and your husband can draw up a separation agreement and this can be ruled by the court, giving it the force of law. Alternatively you can apply to the courts for a judicial separation if you fulfil the criteria set down in the 1989 Act.

Q. *Can you tell me how much maintenance is and whether a child's father should contribute towards the costs of childcare? I received €130 per week from my daughter's father but, since she has started big school, he has deducted €30. I still have the cost of after-school care.*

A. There is no set scale for maintenance. It depends on the parents' means and requirements, and the needs of the children. If your husband was paying maintenance under a court order, he is not entitled to vary the order without returning to court. If he was paying maintenance voluntarily, you should discuss the matter with him. If you are in need and you believe he can afford to pay more but he refuses to do so, you can apply to court for a maintenance order.

Q. *If a divorce is not contested – that is we have reached an agreement suitable to both of us – do we both still have to be represented by barristers? Should all papers be drafted, agreed and signed before the court case?*

A. No. Yes.

Q. *We have been married for only 11 weeks, but almost from the start knew it was not meant to be. Stupid I know, but is there any way out for such a short-lived marriage?*

A. Just because you have decided after a short period that you should not have got married does not mean that you are entitled to a decree of nullity. However, if you believe there was a defect in the consent for the marriage, you should apply for a decree of nullity now. If your marriage is ruled valid, you can apply for a decree of judicial separation after a year, unless there are exceptional circumstances which permit an earlier application. A divorce requires separation for four of the previous five years.

Q. *I'm a US citizen. My ex-husband lives in Ireland and filed for divorce there without informing me. He stated that we had been separated for four years, though we had only been apart for three years. I never received anything official from the court, only a copy of the decree from his attorney.*

A. Separation does not necessarily mean living in separate houses; it can also mean living apart but under the same roof. It may be difficult to prove that you and your husband were having a marital relationship within the four years before his divorce application. If you think you can prove it, you should contact the relevant court and inform the registrar. By the way, if your ex-husband knew your address, he should have served the divorce application papers on you. You should contact an Irish solicitor to confirm the validity of the divorce decree.

Q. *My brother's wife is seeking a legal separation. If that should occur, would I have any rights to see his children who are my nephews and nieces?*

A. Any relative of a child may apply to the court for permission to seek access to that child. The court will take into account the applicant's connection with the child, the risk of disruption to the child's life and the views of the child's guardian.

Q. *My partner and I are not married to each other but we have a five-year-old son. My partner now wishes to assign all his assets to our son but, as he is in mid-divorce from his wife, this is very difficult. What are our son's inheritance rights at present?*

A. If a husband disposes of his assets in order to deprive his wife of what the court may consider to be her share, that disposition may be set aside. The court would look with suspicion on any attempt by a party to a divorce application to divest themselves of all their assets. The needs of all your partner's children will be taken into account by the court when dividing the marital assets. Marital and non-marital children have identical rights to their parents' estates. If your partner died without making a will and before the divorce, his wife and all his children – marital or non-marital – would have a right to share his estate. You would have no automatic right to a share. The situation would be more complicated if your partner had made a will. You should also be aware that remarriage would normally invalidate all previous wills.

Q. *My partner has recently obtained a judicial separation. Next April, it will be four years since he moved out of the family home. Will he then be entitled to a divorce or does he have to wait four years from the date of the judicial separation? Now that he has a judicial separation, will he automatically get a divorce without having to file papers again?*

A. He can apply for a divorce if he has been separated from his wife for four of the past five years. He will have to file a separate application for the divorce, but the judicial separation arrangements will be taken into account by the court.

Q. *I live in the US and have three questions. If a person is legally separated and all issues are settled, how long does it take to obtain a divorce once it has been filed with the courts? Would either or both parties need to be present? Does Ireland recognize a foreign divorce obtained in Mexico or Haiti?*

A. Waiting times vary, but there is currently a waiting list of about four months for uncontested divorce cases in Dublin, according to the Circuit Court family law office. Normally both parties are required to be in court but in certain circumstances where both parties are agreed on all matters, it may be possible for just one spouse to be present. A foreign divorce will be recognised in Ireland if one or both parties were domiciled in the country where the divorce was granted, and the divorce was recognised as valid in that country.

Q. *If a wife leaves the family home due to unacceptable*

*behaviour, such as her husband's alcohol dependence, are
her legal rights to the family home adversely affected?*

A. Desertion might adversely affect a spouse's right to the
family home, but leaving the home for good and sufficient
reason would not be considered desertion.

Q. *Have you come across any instances where a father was
granted custody of a small child, instead of the mother?*

A. Men do obtain custody, but it is fairly rare in practice.
The Irish courts have ruled that, where a child is very young
(all things being equal), a mother should have custody.

Q. *What is the legal definition of a minor? Does a child have
to abide by a separation agreement to see one of his parents
at the weekend, even if the child is not willing to?*

A. The legal definition of a minor is a person under 18 years
old, but if a child of, say, 16 or 17 refuses to see a parent,
there is very little anyone can do. However, in many
separation cases, one parent will claim that a young child of,
say, 8 or 9 does not wish to see the other parent. Sometimes
that can just be the custodial parent applying pressure on the
child. The courts are required to do what is best for the child
and will take a dim view of a parent applying pressure on a
child to defeat the other parent's right to access.

Q. *I am going through a divorce. We have four sons, three of
them over 18 and working. Do I have to pay maintenance for
them? My wife also says she wants half my pension which is
my only income. How much is she allowed of that pension?*

A. The court may order maintenance for dependent children
up to the age of 18, or 23 if in full-time education. There is
no specific rule about the division of a pension. All your

assets and income – and all your wife's assets and income – are taken into account by the court in deciding the issue of maintenance or pension adjustment. If your circumstances later change, you can apply to the court for a variation.

Q. *I had a little boy six years ago but his father and I didn't stay together. My ex now wants to take our son on a two-week holiday. I said that was too long but my ex said he was taking him, no matter what. Can he take our son on holiday without my permission?*

A. The situation depends on a number of matters. Is he a joint guardian of the child? If not, you are entitled to make all the decisions about the child's upbringing unless a court decides otherwise. However, if your ex-partner has been given access rights by a court, you have no right to change those unilaterally. If you are unhappy about the situation, you can apply to the court for a variation of the access arrangements.

Q. *I was granted a judicial separation in 1997, and was awarded maintenance and the family home. I was divorced in 2000. My ex-husband has now threatened to stop paying maintenance because his daughter has no desire to see him. Is he within his rights to do this? Will I have to go back to the courts? Also, I'm earning more money now than I was in 1997. Can this be taken into account?*

A. Your husband is not entitled to vary a maintenance order without your agreement or a court order. If there is an access order for the children, you are not entitled to vary it without agreement or a court order. Your current income and outgoings will be taken into account if your ex-husband applies for a variation of the maintenance order, as will his.

Q. *I lost contact with my husband years ago and don't know* *where he lives. Can I still get a divorce?*

A. Your solicitor should ask the court for directions as to the steps you should take to trace him (such as advertising in newspapers in the area where he might live) in order to serve him with the divorce application. If the court believes it is impossible to trace him, it may allow you to proceed with your application anyway.

Q. *If a couple got married abroad, and later got married in Ireland, would the Irish marriage be void, on the basis that there was an existing valid marriage (albeit to each other)? The foreign marriage was a civil ceremony, and the Irish wedding was a Catholic marriage, with the civil register signed. They have two marriage certificates.*

A. If the couple were already validly married when they went through the ceremony in Ireland, the civil element of the Irish ceremony would be of no effect. However, they would still be validly married under the law of the foreign country and therefore not entitled to a decree of nullity (unless there were other reasons for such a decree).

Q. *My husband and I married five years ago in Ireland and have been living in the USA for the past two years. We're separated for almost one year now and wish to file for divorce here in the US. Will this be recognised in Ireland? Could we apply for a divorce in Ireland instead?*

A. If you are domiciled in the USA and obtain a divorce there, it will be recognised in Ireland. Domicile essentially implies a decision to remain in a place permanently; that is decided by a number of factors. You may only obtain a divorce in Ireland if one of you is domiciled in Ireland on the date of institution of proceedings or if either of you has been ordinarily resident in Ireland for one year ending on that date.

Q. *I live in England and my marriage has irretrievably broken down. My wife is still a resident of Ireland, with our children. What is the difference between applying for a divorce in Ireland and England?*

A. I can't advise you on English family law, but there are several websites which deal with it, including that of my colleague Peter Duckworth at www.duckworthlaw.com. Among the main differences are the waiting time for a divorce (four years' separation in Ireland) and the absence of any "clean break" provision in Irish law.

Q. *I am interested in obtaining specific information on divorce in Ireland and would like to contact you to discuss this. I would appreciate if you would let me know your fee structure.*

A. You would need to consult a solicitor first, as the Bar Council forbids barristers to deal directly with members of the public in these matters, or to advertise their fees. A solicitor will be able to give you guidance about the likely level of legal fees, depending on the complexity of the case.

Q. *My mother died seven years ago and my father has now sold the family home in Kerry where I used to live. The house was in my father's name. Does the Family Home Protection Act provide for this kind of situation?*

A. No. The Family Home Protection Act only protects spouses' rights. Your father is entitled to sell his home if he wishes. If your father dies and leaves you nothing in his will, you may consider making an application within six months for proper provision from his estate.

Q. *Our house is registered in joint names. My husband has always paid the mortgage from his own account and somebody mentioned to me recently that, if anything ever* *went wrong between us, I would not have any claim on the house as I am not contributing towards the mortgage.*

A. A spouse may contribute towards the family home in money or "money's worth" (such as staying at home and looking after children or paying other bills). Both are among the many factors taken into account when dividing property in the case of marriage breakdown.

Q. *My partner left the family home three years ago. Just recently we heard that his wife had been saying that he would have to wait a long, long time for a divorce. Can she prevent the divorce in any way? I also read that divorce is not recognised by the Catholic Church. Does that mean that if he divorces, he cannot legally remarry?*

A. Your partner can apply for a divorce when he has been separated from his wife for four of the previous five years. His wife cannot prevent the divorce as long as he fulfils the criteria set down in the Divorce Act. A divorced person may remarry in a civil ceremony, but a Catholic who was validly married may not remarry in the Catholic Church until his or her partner dies. A person who obtains an ecclesiastical nullity decree may marry in church.

Q. *I got a judicial separation three years ago and accepted £20,000 to transfer the ownership of the family home into my husband's sole name. He also took over payment of the mortgage. I assumed the house was worth about £60,000 at the time, but homes in that area now sell for more than €200,000. Can I ask the court to change the agreement?*

A. It appears that you agreed to the division at the time without a property valuation and are now unhappy because the house was worth more than you thought. The court is unlikely to vary the original order unless there was some impediment preventing you receiving proper advice at the time, although case law suggests that a court may vary the settlement on the grounds of the recent rapid rise in house prices.

Q. *My stepfather has applied for a divorce from my mother. The family home and business were originally bought with my mother's money but my stepfather says he's entitled to half of everything. They are planning to sign an agreement splitting everything down the middle. In the meantime, he has refused to leave the family home, and is being abusive and threatening to my mum and brother. What can we do?*

A. A court will not necessarily give "half of everything" to each spouse in a divorce. It depends on a number of factors, including the amount each spouse has contributed towards the property in money or "money's worth". Pending the hearing of the divorce, your mother can consider obtaining a protection, safety or barring order against your stepfather. She should not sign any agreement until she has been properly advised by a good family law solicitor.

Q. *I'm anxious to know approximately how much I'll be entitled to when my divorce comes before the courts in the next few months. I do have my own lawyer, but he says he is not happy about the Circuit Court judge in my area.*

A. It would be unethical for me to advise you when you have a lawyer on record. If you are unhappy with the outcome of your divorce, you can always consider an appeal to the High Court.

Q. *I got married to a Nigerian national last year. I was just 18 and we had known each other only five months. He forced me to arrange the notification, and even while I was making the vows, I just wanted to run away. The other day he punched* *me full force in the face. He claimed to be 18 when we married, but he has admitted to me that his birth cert and passport are fake. I don't even know who I am married to! Do you think I'd be able to get an annulment?*

A. I presume you are no longer living with this man. If you are, you can apply for a barring order on the grounds of his violence. You should report your suspicions to the gardaí immediately. If he gave false information to the registrar, this could be grounds for nullity. Duress would also be grounds for an annulment.

Q. *I am separated from my husband for just over four months and have applied for a decree of a judicial separation. If I get a judicial separation, will this affect my right to apply for a divorce in later years? Also I am considering moving to the north of Ireland with my two young children. Could my husband bring charges of child abduction against me?*

A. A decree of judicial separation will not affect your right to apply for a decree of divorce after four years' separation. If you have joint custody of the children, you must obtain your husband's consent before taking them out of the state to live. If he will not give consent, you can apply to the court for permission to go. The judge's decision will be based on the best interests of the children.

Q. *My husband and I are Irish citizens who married in the Republic of Ireland. We have now moved to Canada to live permanently. Can we file for divorce here or would we have to return to Ireland?*

A. You cannot apply for a divorce in Ireland unless one of you has been ordinarily resident here for 12 months. If you wish to apply for a divorce in Canada, you should consult a Canadian lawyer.

Q. *My wife and I were both 19 at the time of our marriage in 1994 and had only been together for about eight weeks as a couple. She was pregnant when we got married. After a few months, I came home from work one evening and found that my wife had left, taking my daughter with her. She is now living with another man and they have two children. Would I be entitled to a nullity?*

A. The shortness of your relationship with your wife, your respective ages and her pregnancy would certainly be relevant factors in any nullity application. You should consider applying for a nullity with a fallback position of seeking a divorce if the nullity is not granted.

Q. *I am separated nine years from my husband. He now lives in Spain. (I have his address). Can I serve the divorce documents on him in Spain?*

A. You would need to apply to the court for permission to serve the papers on your husband outside the jurisdiction. Your solicitor will advise you of the procedure.

Q. *I am in the process of separating. My daughter, who lives with me, is profoundly mentally and physically handicapped. Someone told me that, if you have a handicapped child, you are entitled to get the house in your sole name. Is this so?*

A. No. If you have custody of the handicapped child, the likelihood is that you will be allowed to remain in the family home until your daughter no longer needs special care, at which stage the property may be sold and the proceeds divided between you and your husband. That would depend on the circumstances at that time.

Q. *I know of a case of two people who were married in a Catholic church in Ireland just 22 days after they met. The* *girl was 23 and on holiday and the man was 29. They married before the new law requiring three months' notice. Are they validly married?*

A. If the couple were free to marry one another, complied with the legal requirements at the time and gave their full consent to the marriage, they are validly married.

Q. *Is it true that a woman who leaves the family home before a separation has been finalised, loses any rights to a share of the family home if it is sold? I have been told that this is classed as deserting the family home.*

A. Desertion may be taken into account by a court when dividing assets, but it does not necessarily mean a woman loses her rights to any share in the family home. Leaving the family home for good reason does not qualify as desertion.

Q. *I am an Irish citizen currently living in the US. My wife is seeking a judicial separation in Ireland. It has now come to my attention that she has got engaged to marry someone else without having any separation or divorce. Can she do that?*

A. Your wife is quite entitled to tell someone that she will marry him in the future. However, she cannot marry anyone else after a judicial separation, as she would still be validly married. She would either need a decree of divorce or nullity – or for you to die.

Q. *My husband has been barred from the family home, which is in joint names. Can I decide to sell the family home after a period of time without a court order or his agreement, as I am now the only occupant of the house?*

A. No.

Appendices

Appendix A

Glossary of Legal Terms

A mensa et thoro: from table and bed (a earlier form of judicial separation).

Abatement: reduction of a legacy in a will.

Access: the right of a person who is not a custodian to see a child.

Action: a civil court proceeding.

Ad litem: (for the suit), the appointment of a person to represent a child in an action.

Adjournment: the postponement of a hearing by a judge.

Adultery: sexual intercourse by a married person with someone other than his or her spouse.

Affidavit of means: sworn statement of financial affairs.

Affidavit of welfare: sworn statement relating to children of a marriage.

Affidavit: a sworn written statement.

Ancillary relief: additional related orders available from the court.

Annulment: declaration by a court that a valid marriage never existed.

Appeal: challenge to a court's finding in a higher court.

Appellant: person who brings an appeal.

Applicant: person who makes an application to a court.

Arrears: overdue payments.

Attachment and committal: bringing a person before a court, with a threat of imprisonment for failure to obey a court order.

Attachment of earnings: deduction of salary at source.

Barring order: order preventing the respondent threatening or molesting another person or entering the applicant's home.

Barrister: specialist lawyer-advocate.

Bigamy: criminal offence of marrying another person while still in a valid marriage.

Canon law: the law of the Catholic Church, promulgated in 1983.

Chambers: a judge's personal rooms, where he may hear matters in private.

Charge: form of security for payment of a debt.

Chattels: household goods.

Child: person under 18.

Child abduction: wrongful removal of a child from its parent, guardian or country of residence.

Circuit Family Court: court above the District Court and below the High Court, with power to grant divorces and judicial separations.

Circuit Judge: judge of the Circuit Court, usually addressed as "My Lord" whether male or female.

Codicil: Addition to a will.

Cohabitation: living together as husband and wife, although not married.

Collusion: unlawful, and usually secret, agreement.

Common law spouses: colloquial term for unmarried partners.

Conciliation: bringing spouses together with a third party to try to resolve differences.

Conjugal rights: the right of one spouse to cohabit with the other.

Consent order: court order agreed between the two sides.

Consummation: completed (as a marriage is completed by sexual intercourse) .

Contempt: wilful disregard of a court order.

Counsel: barrister(s).

Counselling: giving advice with a view to resolving differences.

Counterclaim: respondent's claim against applicant.

Cross-petition: a claim by a respondent against a petitioner.

Custody: care and charge of a child.

Decree: declaration by a court.

Deed of separation: written voluntary agreement by a couple not to cohabit.

Defence: response to claim by applicant.

Defendant: person against whom proceedings are brought.

Defined benefit pension scheme: where retirement benefits are based on an individual's final pay and service with the employer.

Defined contribution pension scheme: where employee and employer contribute to a fluctuating investment fund.

Dependent family member: person under 18 (or 23 if in full-time education) or one who is mentally or physically disabled.

Deponent: person who swears an affidavit.

Desertion: unilateral termination of cohabitation without good reason.

Discovery: sworn disclosure of documents .

District Court: lowest court, with powers to deal with maintenance, barring orders, etc.

District Judge: judge of the District Court, addressed as "Judge."

Divorce: a declaration that a valid marriage has ended and that the parties are free to marry again.

Domicile: established and permanent country of residence.

Duress: threatened or actual force.

Exhibit: item or document produced during court proceedings.

Ex parte: court application made without notice to the other person.

Family home: house in which a married couple usually live or last lived together.

Family law civil bill: initiating document in divorce and judicial separation proceedings.

Guardian: person with right and duty to look after a child.

Hearsay: inadmissible evidence of second-hand reports.

High Court: court above the Circuit Court with full jurisdiction to decide all matters of law and fact.

High Court judges: male and female, normally addressed as "My Lord."

Illegitimate: status of child born outside marriage, abolished in 1987 .

Impotence: inability to have sexual intercourse.

Injunction: court order forbidding or requiring a certain course of action.

Interim: temporary, pending a final decision.

Intestacy: death without a valid will.

Jactitation: false claim to be married to someone.

Judicial separation: court order removing a spouse's duty to cohabit.

Jurisdiction: power of a court to deal with certain matters.

Legal Aid: government scheme providing advice or assistance from a solicitor or barrister at a reduced rate or free.

Lump sum: money paid to spouse in lieu of (or as well as) maintenance.

Marriage: the voluntary union for life of one man and one woman to the exclusion of all others.

Maintenance: periodic payments by one spouse to the other.

Mediation: arbitration with the aim of reaching agreement on separation.

Nullity: annulment, a declaration by a court that a valid marriage never existed.

Orse: otherwise known as.

Parent: father or mother of a child, whether married or not.

Partition: division of land or property.

Paternity: fatherhood, which may be established by DNA testing.

Pension adjustment: order for payment of part of all of one spouse's pension to the other spouse.

Periodical payments: maintenance payments.

Petition: written application to the court for judicial remedy, such as nullity.

Petitioner: person issuing petition.

Pleadings: written allegations or claims delivered by one spouse to the other.

Property adjustment: court order transferring property from one spouse to another or varying ownership of property.

Protection order: temporary court order preventing a person from threatening, molesting or pestering another, pending a barring application.

Reply: answer of a plaintiff to a defence or counterclaim.

Reserved costs: apportionment of payment of legal fees to be decided at a later stage.

Residence: place where a person usually – but not necessarily permanently – lives.

Respondent: person who responds to a court application.

Safety order: an order preventing the use or threat of violence against an applicant, or molesting or frightening the applicant.

Secured payment: court order ensuring payment of maintenance by one spouse to the other.

Separation agreement: a voluntary agreement between two

spouses to live apart.

Service: delivery of court documents by one party to the other, personally or by post.

Settlement: agreed compromise of proceedings.

Solicitor: general lawyer who may deal directly with the public.

Spouse: husband or wife.

Summons: written command to a person to appear in court.

Testamentary capacity: legal ability to make a will.

Testator/Testatrix: person who makes a will.

Tort: non-contractual breach of duty.

Undertaking: enforceable promise.

Undue influence: unfair pressure which may invalidate a contract.

Variation: alteration of term of order.

Void: without legal effect.

Voidable: capable of being set aside.

Appendix B

Irish Family Law Legislation

Property (Ireland) Act 1865: permitted a wife to sue her husband in tort if separated or deserted.

Partition Acts 1868 and 1876: allowed court to divide up property between spouses.

Matrimonial Causes and Marriage Law (Ireland) (Amendment) Act 1870: required rules of civil nullity to approximate to Church rules.

Married Women's Property Act 1882: allowed a wife to hold property in her own name. Replaced by:

Married Women's Status Act 1957: made wives liable for their own debts and breaches of duty. Allowed the court to decide disputes between spouses over title to property.

Guardianship of Infants Act 1964: gave parents the right to be joint guardians of their children and allowed the courts to make decisions on custody and access.

Succession Act 1965: reformed the law relating to the estates of deceased persons, especially the administration and distribution of property on intestacy. Specified the shares of spouses and children on intestacy.

Marriages Act 1972: raised the minimum marriage age to 16 for boys and girls, retrospectively validated so-called "Lourdes marriages".

Maintenance Orders Act 1974: allowed the reciprocal enforcement of maintenance orders between the Republic of Ireland, Northern Ireland, England and Wales and Scotland.

Family Law (Maintenance of Spouses and Children) Act 1976: provided for periodical payments by one spouse to another in cases of failure to provide reasonable maintenance, with deductions of earnings at source and barring orders.

Family Home Protection Act 1976: required prior written consent of spouse for sale of family home or chattels.

Courts Act 1980: widened the Circuit Court's jurisdiction in family law matters.

Luxembourg Convention 1980: European convention on enforcement of decisions concerning custody of children and restoration of custody.

Hague Convention 1980: European convention to secure the return of children wrongfully removed from one State to another and to ensure custody and access orders are respected in contracting States.

Family Law Act 1981: abolished actions for enticement of spouse and breach of promise to marry. Court can decide disputes over gifts to formerly engaged couples.

Family Law (Protection of Spouses and Children) Act 1981: gave the Circuit and District Courts power to grant barring and protection orders. (Repealed by Domestic Violence Act 1996)

Domicile and Recognition of Foreign Divorces Act 1986: gave wives independent domiciles from their husbands, recognised divorces granted where either spouse was domiciled.

Status of Children Act 1987: abolished status of illegitimacy and amended law on maintenance and succession for non-marital children. Allowed an unmarried father to apply to be his child's guardian. Provided for blood tests to establish paternity.

Family Law Act 1988: abolished actions for the restitution of conjugal rights. (Act is just 30 words long!)

Children Act 1989: gave powers to health boards in relation to care of children.

Judicial Separation and Family Law Reform Act 1989: amended the grounds for judicial separation, facilitated reconciliation between estranged spouses and provided for ancillary orders such as maintenance, property adjustment and custody of children.

Child Care Act 1991: gave powers to health boards to care for children who were ill-treated, neglected or sexually abused.

Child Abduction and Enforcement of Custody Orders Act 1991: dealt with wrongful retention of children.

Maintenance Act 1994: gave effect to EU convention on simplified procedures for recovering maintenance payments from other countries.

Family Law Act 1995: raised the minimum age for marriage to 18 and required 3 months' written notice to local registrar of marriages, abolished petitions for jactitation of marriage (falsely claiming to be married to someone), provided for declarations of marital status and amended the 1989 Act by regulating ancillary orders after judicial separation or foreign divorce.

Domestic Violence Act 1996: replaced 1981 Act and extended safety, barring and protection orders to non-spouses, gave health boards powers to apply for orders, allowed arrest without warrant for breach.

Family Law (Divorce) Act 1996: permitted divorce and remarriage, with all ancillary orders.

Registration of Births Act 1996: amended the law on the registration and re-registration of births.

Children Act 1997: permitted natural fathers to become guardians by consent, provided for children's views to be considered in guardianship, access and custody matters, allowed parents to have joint custody.

Family Law (Miscellaneous Provisions) Act 1997: amended the law in relation to notification of intention to marry, barring orders, powers of attorney and distribution of disclaimed estates.

European Council Regulation 1347/2000: allowed – subject to certain conditions – the mutual recognition in all EU

Member States (except Denmark) of court orders relating to divorce, legal separation, nullity or child custody.

Children Act 2001: authorised courts to order health boards to convene a family conference where a child requires special care or protection. The health board can apply for a care order or supervision order if necessary.

(The texts of all these Acts are available online at http://indigo.ie/~kwood/acts.htm)

Appendix C

Family Law (Divorce) Act 1996

PART I – PRELIMINARY

Section 1(1) The short title of the Act is the Family Law (Divorce) Act.

Section 1(2) The Act came into operation on February 27th 1997.

Section 2(1) Interpretation section.

Section 3 Repeal of section14 (2) of the Censorship of Publications Act 1929, restricting the media's right to publish full details of divorce, nullity or separation cases.

Section 4 Administration of the Act is to be financed by the Oireachtas.

PART II – OBTAINING A DECREE OF DIVORCE

Section 5

(1) The court may grant a divorce where it is satisfied that:

    (a) when the proceedings began, the spouses had lived apart for at least four of the preceding five years,

(b) there is no reasonable prospect of reconciliation and

(c) there has been (or will be) proper provision for the spouses and dependent children

(2) The court may give directions about the dependent children's welfare, custody and access.

Section 6

(1) The person applying for the divorce is called the applicant.

(2) Before proceedings begin, the applicant's solicitor must discuss:

(a) the possibility of reconciliation and provide the names and addresses of people qualified to help reconcile the couple,

(b) the possibility of mediation to help the couple agree the basis of their separation or divorce, and provide the names and addresses of qualified mediators, and

(c) the possibility of a written separation agreement.

(3) If the couple are not judicially separated, the applicant's solicitor must tell him about judicial separation as an alternative to divorce.

(4)(a) Any solicitor acting for the applicant must sign a certificate confirming he has complied with sub-sections (2) and, if necessary, (3) and must hand in that certificate with the original petition, or else the court may adjourn the application.

(b) The solicitor must leave a copy of the certificate with any copy of the petition served on anyone else or left in a court office.

(5) The certificate must be in the form required by the rules of court.

(6) The minister may make regulations for the estab-lishment of a register of professional organisations whose members are qualified to help reconcile spouses. The register would give the names of members of the organisations and procedures for regular updating of the membership lists.

Section 7

(1) The spouse who is not the applicant is called the respondent.

(2) As soon as any solicitor acting for the respondent receives instructions, he must discuss with her:

    (a) the possibility of reconciliation and give her the names and addresses of people qualified to help reconcile the couple,

    (b) the possibility of mediation to help bring about a separation or divorce on an agreed basis, and give her the names and addresses of qualified mediators, and

    (c) the possibility of a written separation agreement.

(3) If the couple are not already judicially separated, the respondent's solicitor must tell her about judicial separation as an alternative to divorce.

(4)(a) Any solicitor acting for the applicant must sign a certificate confirming he has complied with subsections (2) and, if necessary, (3) and must hand in that document with the original petition, or else the court may adjourn the application.

    (b) The solicitor must leave a copy of the certificate with any copy of the petition served on anyone else or left in a court office.

(5) The certificate must be in the form required by the rules of court.

Section 8

(1) If both spouses wish, the court may adjourn divorce proceedings at any time, to allow the couple to consider reconciliation.

(2) If the court believes the spouses can't be reconciled, it may adjourn proceedings (if both spouses wish) to let them try and reach agreement on some, or all, of the terms of the proposed divorce.

(3) If proceedings are adjourned for talks on reconciliation

or divorce terms, and either spouse wants them resumed, the court will resume the proceedings.

(4) The powers conferred by this section are additional to any other power the court may have to adjourn proceedings.

(5) Where the court does adjourn proceedings under this section, it may advise the couple to seek the help of a third party.

Section 9

If the couple seek assistance for the purpose of reconciliation or to reach agreement on the terms of a divorce or separation, any oral or written communication between either spouse and a third party (whether or not the other spouse knows about it), and any record of such a communication by either spouse or the third party, will not be admissible in evidence.

Section 10

(1) A decree of divorce dissolves the marriage and the spouses are free to remarry.

(2) A divorce decree does not affect the right of a father or mother to be joint guardians of their child.

PART III – PRELIMINARY AND ANCILLARY ORDERS DURING OR
AFTER DIVORCE PROCEEDINGS

Section 11

Before the court grants a divorce, it may make one or more of the following orders without an application under the relevant Act:

    (a) a safety order, barring order, temporary barring order or protection order,

    (b) an order for the custody, access or maintenance of a dependent child,

    (c) an order to protect the family home, its contents or

any money from its sale.

Section 12

(1) The court may order either spouse to pay maintenance for the other spouse and any dependent children from the date of the application until the court's final decision. Alternatively, a spouse may be ordered to pay a lump sum or sums.

(2) The court may decide appropriate terms and conditions for such payments.

Section 13

(1) When the court grants the divorce, on an application by either spouse (or on behalf of a dependent child), the court may make any of the following orders during the lifetime of either spouse:

   (a) a periodical payments order; that is an order:
      (i)   for one spouse to make payments to the other, as often as, and for as long as, the court orders (See section 13(4)) or
      (ii) for either spouse to make payments to another person for the benefit of a dependent child, as often, and for as long as, the court orders (See section 13(4))
   (b) a secured periodical payments order, that is an order:
      (i)   for one spouse to secure payments to the other to the court's satisfaction or
      (ii) for either spouse to secure payments to another person for a dependent child, to the court's satisfaction
   (c) a lump sum payments order, that is an order:
      (i)   for one spouse to pay a lump sum (or sums) to the other at specified time(s), or
      (ii) for either spouse to pay a lump sum (or sums) to another person for a dependent child at specified time(s)

(2) The court may order a spouse to pay a lump sum to:

    (a) the other spouse to meet any liabilities or expenses reasonably incurred before that spouse applied for a periodical payments order or

    (b) a specified person to meet any liabilities or expenses reasonably incurred before a periodical payments application was made on behalf of a dependent child.

(3) The court may order that the lump sum be paid by specified instalments, and that payment be secured.

(4) Periodical payments shall not start before the application for the divorce and shall not continue beyond the death of either spouse or any dependent child in whose favour the order is made.

(5)(a) Periodical payments shall stop when a spouse remarries, except for any arrears due.

    (b) If a spouse remarries after the divorce, the court will not make a periodical payments order in his or her favour.

(6)(a) At the same time as a court makes a periodical payments order, it shall – subject to any secured order – make an attachment of earnings order if the spouse earns wages. (See section 10(2) of the Family Law (Maintenance of Spouses and Children) Act 1976)

    (b) Before making an attachment of earnings order, the court shall take into account the spouse's views in relation to:

    (c) (i) whether he is paid "earnings"– that is wages, salary (including fees, bonus or commission) or pension and

        (ii) whether he would make the payments without such an order.

    (d) References to a periodical payments order include references to an order which has been appealed or varied (See section 22).

Section 14

(1) At any time after granting a divorce, on an application by either spouse (or on behalf of a dependent child), the court may – during the lifetime of either spouse – make a property adjustment order providing for one or more of the following:

(a) the transfer of property by either spouse to the other spouse, to a dependent child or to another person for the benefit of a dependent child

(b) the satisfactory settlement of specified property for the benefit of the other spouse and/or any dependent child

(c) the variation of any pre-marriage or post-marriage settlement made on the couple (including any settlement in a will), for the benefit of either spouse and/or any dependent child

(d) the extinguishment or reduction of the interest of either spouse under such a settlement.

(2) The court may restrict or refuse to allow future variations of orders made under paragraphs (b), (c) or (d).

(3) If a spouse remarries after obtaining a divorce, the court will not make a property adjustment order in his or her favour.

(4) Where a property adjustment order relates to land, the registrar or clerk of the court shall lodge a certified copy of the order in the Land Registry or Registry of Deeds.

(5) Where:

(a) a person is ordered to execute a deed or document in relation to land and

(b) refuses or fails to do so, (or if the court considers it necessary),

the court may order another person to execute the deed or document, and that execution shall be valid.

(6) The court will apportion any costs in relation to a property adjustment order between the spouses.

(7) If a spouse remarries after a divorce, the court will not make a property adjustment order in relation to the home where that spouse lives with his or her new partner.

Section 15

(1) When the court grants a divorce, on an application by either spouse (or on behalf of a dependent child), the court may – during the lifetime of either spouse – make any of the following:

    (a) an order:
        (i) giving one spouse the right to live in the family home for life or any other period, to the exclusion of the other spouse or
        (ii) directing the sale of the family home and the division of the proceeds between the spouses and anyone else with an interest in the property (See section 15(2) and section 15(3)).
    (b) an order deciding the ownership of any property,
    (c) an order dispensing with the consent of a spouse who refuses to agree to the sale of the home, an order to protect the home, an order relating to arrears of mortgage or rent, an order restricting the disposal of household chattels,
    (d) a safety, barring, interim barring or protection order on the application of a spouse of the respondent, person who lives with the respondent, parent of the respondent, co-habitee or health board,
    (e) an order for the partition of the property,
    (f) a custody, access or other order relating to the welfare of a child.

(2) In relation to orders under subsection (1)(a), the court shall consider the welfare of the spouses and any dependent children and, in particular, shall take into consideration:

    (a) that a couple cannot live together after they have divorced and
    (b) that dependent children and dependent spouses should be provided with proper and secure accommodation.

(3) If a spouse remarries after a divorce, subsection (1)(a) does not apply to a family home where that spouse lives with

his or her new partner.

Section 16

(1) At any time after the court grants a divorce, on an application by either spouse (or on behalf of a dependent child) during the lifetime of either spouse, if the court considers that:

    (a) the financial security of the applicant spouse or child can be improved or

    (b) compensation should be made to the applicant or child for giving up a benefit, such as a pension,

the court may make a financial compensation order requiring the other spouse to do one or more of the following:

    (i) take out a life insurance policy for the benefit of the applicant or child,

    (ii) assign some or all of the benefit of an existing life insurance policy to the applicant or child,

    (iii) continue to pay life insurance premiums. (See section 16(2)(d))

(2)(a) The court can make a financial compensation order as well as (or instead of) all or part of the orders under sections 13, 14, 15 or 17, but it must take into account whether, in the circumstances, proper provision exists (or can be made) for the spouse and child concerned.

    (b) A financial compensation order ceases to apply to an applicant who dies or remarries.

    (c) The court shall not make a financial compensation order in favour of a spouse who has remarried.

    (d) In relation to a life insurance policy, the court may vary any order concerning the disposal of:

        (i) an amount equal to the accumulated value of a policy taken out under subsection (1)(i) or

        (ii) the interest or part-interest in a policy under subsection (1)(ii).

Section 17

(1) Pension adjustment orders interpretation section.

(2) If either spouse is a member of a retirement benefit scheme, either may apply at any time after a divorce decree (during the member's lifetime) for an order to pay:

> (a) the member's spouse or, in case of death, the personal representative or
>
> (b) anyone specified, for the benefit of a dependent child

all (or part) of the benefit which has accrued at the time of the divorce decree. The application may also be made by someone on behalf of a dependent child. The order will specify:

> (i) the period of reckonable service of the member before the divorce and
>
> (ii) the percentage of the benefits accrued during that period to be paid to the applicant.

(3) On application by either spouse (or a person on behalf of a dependent child) within one year of the divorce decree, the court may order that all (or a specified percentage) of any death-in-service benefit be paid on the member's death to:

> (a) the other spouse and/or
>
> (b) anyone specified, for the benefit of a dependent child.

The court will decide what share each applicant is to receive.

(4) Where a pension adjustment order is made, and payment of the retirement benefit has not yet started, the applicant will be entitled to an equal amount of money from the scheme (a "transfer amount"), as calculated by the scheme's trustees.

(5) Where a pension adjustment order is made, and payment of the retirement benefit has not yet started:

> (a) on application by the spouse in whose favour the order was made and
>
> (b) after being provided with any information required

by that spouse

the scheme's trustees shall use the transfer amount either:

    (i) to provide the spouse with a benefit of the same actuarial value (if the trustees and spouse agree), or

   (ii) to make a payment, at the spouse's discretion, to:

        (I) another occupational pension scheme of which the trustees agree to accept the payment or

       (II) pay off any money owed by the trustees under an approved insurance policy.

(6) Where the pension scheme is a *defined contribution* scheme, and a spouse has not applied for a transfer amount, the trustees may, if they see fit, make a payment:

    (a) to another occupational pension scheme where the trustees agree to accept the payment or

    (b) to pay off any money owed by the trustees under an insurance policy.

(7) Where:

    (a) a pension adjustment order is made and

    (b) the member dies before payment of benefits has started,

the trustees must – within three months of the death – pay an equal transfer amount to the person in whose favour the order was made, calculated in accordance with relevant guidelines.

(8) Where:

    (a) a pension adjustment order is made and

    (b) the member leaves the scheme (other than dying),

the trustees may apply the transfer amount in accordance with the guidelines either:

    (i) to provide a benefit of the same value under the same scheme (if the trustees and spouse agree) or

    (ii) to make a payment
        (I) to another occupational pension scheme
            which will accept the payment or
        (II) to pay off any money due under an in-
            surance policy,

whichever the trustees prefer.

    (9) Where:
      (a) a pension adjustment order is made and
      (b) the recipient spouse dies before payment of benefits
          has started,

within three months of the death, the trustees shall pay an
equal transfer amount to the spouse's personal representative.

    (10) Where:
      (a) a pension adjustment order is made and
      (b) the recipient dies *after* payment of benefits has
          started,

the trustees shall pay to the personal representative – within
three months of the death – an amount equal to the value of
the balance of the benefit which would have otherwise been
paid to the spouse during the member's lifetime.

    (11) Where:
      (a) a pension adjustment order is made in favour of a
          child and
      (b) the child dies before payment of benefits has started,

that part of the order shall have no further effect.

    (12) Where:
      (a) a pension adjustment or death-in-service order is
          made in relation to an occupational pension scheme
          and
      (b) the trustees of the scheme have not transferred the
          amount concerned and,
      (c) after the order was made, the member leaves the
          scheme,

within a year of his leaving, the trustees shall notify the clerk
of the court and the other spouse.

    (13) Where the trustees make a transfer under subsections

6 or 8, they must notify the member's spouse (or other person concerned) and the court, giving particulars of the scheme and the amount transferred.

(14) Where a pension adjustment or death-in-service order is made, the benefit (or transfer amount) is payable out of the scheme concerned and must be paid in accordance with the rules of the scheme, unless the order says otherwise.

(15) Where a pension adjustment order is made, the amount of retirement benefit payable to the member shall be reduced by the amount of benefits payable under the order.

    (16)(a)   Where a death-in-service order is made, the amount of benefit payable to the member is reduced by the amount of death benefit payable to the spouse.

        (b)   Where a pension adjustment order is made and the member dies before payment of benefits begins, the amount of death benefit payable to the member is reduced by the amount payable under subsection 7.

(17) Where a pension adjustment order is made and the trustees make a payment under any one of subsections 5 to 10, they do not have to make any further payments under any other of those subsections.

(18) A person who applies for a pension adjustment or death-in-service order, or a change in an existing order, must notify the trustees, and the court shall take note of the representations of the trustees, the member and anyone else specified by the court before making the order.

(19) A death-in-service order shall cease to have any effect on the death or remarriage of the member's spouse or child.

(20) At any time after the making of a pension adjustment order, the court may give the trustees directions which contravene the scheme rules or the Pensions Act 1990. The trustees shall not be liable for any loss or damage caused by their compliance with the court's directions.

(21) The registrar or clerk of the court must serve the

trustees with a copy of any pension adjustment order.

(22)(a)   The court will decide whether the costs incurred by the trustees (in relation to making representations, obeying court directions, making calculations or complying with a pension adjustment order) should be met by the member, the other spouse or both of them. If there is no order, the costs are shared equally.

(b)   If a person fails to pay his share of the costs, the trustees may apply to the court for the share to be deducted from any pension adjustment or death-in-service payment.

(23)(a)   No pension adjustment order shall be made in favour of a spouse who has remarried.

(b)   A pension adjustment order may be made instead of, or as well as, any periodical payments, lump sum, property adjustment, financial compensation or family home order. Before making a pension adjustment order, the court must decide whether proper provision has been made for the spouse and children by the other orders.

(24) Section 54 of the Pension Act 1990 (dealing with the disclosure of information about schemes) shall apply, with any necessary modifications, to a scheme where a member is involved in divorce proceedings.

(25) The court may direct the trustees within a certain time to calculate:

(a)   the value and amount of the retirement or death-in-service benefit that had accrued when the order was made (or the benefit that would have been payable if there had been no divorce) and

(b)   the amount of death-in-service benefit payable.

If either spouse (or anyone else concerned) requests the information, the court must direct the trustees to provide it.

(26) An order under this section may restrict or exclude any future variation.

Section 18

(1) Where a divorced spouse dies, on application by the other spouse within six months of the grant of probate, the court may order that the applicant be provided for out of the estate, taking into account the rights of anyone else with an interest in the estate. The court must specify in the order that the deceased spouse did not make proper provision for the applicant within his lifetime under sections 13–17, having regard to his circumstances, for some reason other than the applicant's conduct.

(2) The court shall not make an order under this section for someone who has remarried.

(3) Before making any order, the court shall consider all the circumstances, including:

> (a) any property adjustment order or lump sum payments to the applicant
>
> (b) any bequest made to the applicant by the deceased spouse.

(4) Taking into account any lump sum or property adjustment order, the applicant may not receive more than he or she would have been entitled to under the Succession Act if there had been no divorce. The value of any lump sum or property adjustment order is taken as its value on the date of the original order.

(5) The applicant must give notice of the application to the spouse of the deceased person and to anyone else the court may direct, and the court shall take account of their views.

(6) The personal representative of the deceased spouse shall make a reasonable attempt to inform any potential applicant about the death of the deceased spouse and, if an application is made, the personal representative shall not dispose of any of the estate without the court's permission until the court has ruled on the application.

(7) Where the personal representative of a deceased spouse has given notice to the surviving spouse and:

(a) the spouse intends to apply for an order under this section,

(b) the spouse has already applied for an order or

(c) an order has already been made,

the surviving spouse must notify the personal representative within a month of the notice or else the assets may be distributed among those entitled to them.

(8) In the case of such a distribution, the personal representative shall not be liable to the surviving spouse for those assets.

(9) Even if the assets have been distributed, the surviving spouse may still try and recover them.

(10) At any time after the court grants a decree of divorce, it may order (on the application of either spouse) that neither spouse be entitled to apply for an order under this section.

Section 19

(1) At any time after the court makes an order for secured periodical payments, a lump sum or property adjustment, it may order the sale of property in which either of the spouses has an interest.

(2) The court will not order the sale of a family home where it has already ordered that a spouse should have the right to occupy the home.

(3)(a) An order for sale may contain other appropriate provisions.

(b) An order for sale may also specify:

(i) the manner and conditions of sale,

(ii) the person(s) to whom the property must be offered,

(iii) the date when the order is to come into effect,

(iv) payment(s) to a specified person from the proceeds of sale, and

(v) the division of the proceeds.

(4) Periodical payments to a spouse out of the proceeds of sale shall cease on the death or remarriage of that spouse,

except for any arrears due.

(5) The court must take note of representations by anyone (other than the spouse) who has an interest in the property or the proceeds of sale.

(6) This section does not apply to a family home where a divorced spouse ordinarily lives with his or her new spouse.

Section 20

(1) The court must ensure that, in all the circumstances, the spouses and dependent children are properly provided for when making an order under sections 12, 13, 14, 15 (1)(a), 16, 17, 18 or 22.

(2) In particular, the court shall also consider:

- (a) the income, earning capacity, property and other financial resources of each spouse at the time or in the foreseeable future,
- (b) the financial needs, obligations and responsibilities of each spouse at the time or in the foreseeable future (whether in the case of remarriage or not),
- (c) the standard of living enjoyed by the family before the proceedings began or the spouses started to live apart,
- (d) the age of the spouses, duration of marriage and length of time they lived together,
- (e) any physical or mental disability of either spouse,
- (f) the contribution which each spouse has made (or is likely to make) to the welfare of the family, including contributions to the income, earning capacity, property and financial resources of the other spouse, and any contribution made by looking after the home or caring for the family,
- (g) the effect of marital responsibility on the earning capacity of either spouse while they were living together, and particularly the degree to which a spouse's future earning capacity was affected by giving up the possibility of paid work to look after

the home or care for the family,

(h) any income or benefits to which either spouse is statutorily entitled,

(i) the conduct of either of the spouses, if it would be unjust, in all the circumstances, to disregard such conduct,

(j) the accommodation needs of either spouse,

(k) the value to either spouse of any benefit (such as a pension) which would be lost because of the divorce and

(l) the rights of anyone else, including a new husband or wife.

(3) The court shall consider the terms of any separation agreement still in force.

(4) In relation to any dependent child, the court shall particularly consider:

(a) his financial needs,

(b) his income, earning capacity, property or other financial resources,

(c) any physical or mental disability,

(d) any income or benefits to which he is statutorily entitled,

(e) the parents' proposed education or training of the child,

(f) the matters specified in paragraphs (a), (b) and (c) of subsection (2) and subsection (3) and

(g) his accommodation needs.

(5) The court shall not make any order under subsection (1) unless it would be in the interests of justice to do so.

Section 21

(1) In an order for periodical payments, the court may direct that:

(a) payments be backdated to the date proceedings began,

(b) any retrospective payments be paid in a lump sum

by a set date,
(c) any payments made between the start of proceedings and date of the decree be deducted from the lump sum.

(2) The right to order retrospective payments does not affect the court's right to order payment of any other lump sum.

Section 22

(1) This section applies to the following orders:
(a) maintenance pending suit,
(b) periodical payments,
(c) secured periodical payments,
(d) lump sums by instalments or by secured instalments,
(e) the settlement of specified property and variation or extinguishment of any settlement,
(f) a right of residence in the family home or for the sale of the family home and division of the proceeds,
(g) financial compensation,
(h) pension adjustment and
(i) orders made under this section.
(2) Subject to specified restrictions, on application by:
(a) either spouse,
(b) on the death of either spouse, by anyone else with a sufficient interest or on behalf of a dependent child or
(c) by a new spouse in the case of remarriage,
in the light of changed circumstances or new evidence, the court may temporarily or permanently change, suspend, revive or discharge an order, and may require a person to give up property obtained under such an order.

(3) Periodical payments shall cease when a child reaches the age of 18 (or 23 if in full-time education) and the court shall discharge such an order if the child has ceased to be dependent.

(4) The power of the court to change an order settling

property, or extinguishing or varying a settlement (subject to any restriction in the order) is a power

> (a) to vary the settlement in favour of anyone or to extinguish or reduce anyone's interest and,
> (b) in the light of such variation, to make any appropriate additional provision (including another property adjustment or lump sum order)

and section 19 will apply to any variation of an order under subsection (2) and to any property adjustment order.

(5) The court shall not vary an order settling property, or extinguishing or varying a settlement, if it believes such a variation would prejudice the interests of anyone who:

> (a) has acquired a right or interest as a result of the original order and
> (b) is not a spouse or dependent child.

(6) This section will apply to any legal documents executed as a result of any variation orders.

(7) Where the court varies a property adjustment order relating to land, the registrar or clerk of the court shall lodge a certified copy in the Land Registry or Registry of Deeds.

Section 23

The court will disregard the conduct of spouses when deciding whether to:

> (a) include a dependent child in an order for maintenance pending suit,
> (b) make an order for periodical payments, secured periodical payments or a lump sum to a dependent child,
> (c) vary such orders.

Section 24

(1) The court may order that payments shall be made by a specified method and subject to appropriate terms and conditions.

(2) This section applies to an order under:

(a) section 11 (2)(b) of the 1964 Act (maintenance for an infant)
(b) section 5, 5A or 7 of the 1976 Act (maintenance of spouses and dependent children and interim orders)
(c) section 7, 8 or 24 of the 1995 Act (maintenance pending suit, periodical payments, lump sum orders and maintenance pending relief) and
(d) section 12, 13, 19 or 22 of this Act (financial or property orders).

Section 25

Where there is an appeal against any such order (except in relation to lump sum payments, property sale or residence orders), there will be no stay on the order unless the court that made the order (or the appeal court) rules otherwise.

Section 26

(1) Where an order is in force for:
(a) maintenance, variation of maintenance or interim maintenance under the 1976 Act,
(b) periodical or lump sum payments, property adjustment, sale, transfer or partition, the right to occupy the family home or guardianship under the 1989 Act,
(c) periodical or lump sum payments, property adjustment, sale, transfer or partition, the right to occupy the family home, guardianship, pension adjustment, extinction of succession rights or financial compensation under the 1995 Act

the court may discharge the order if the spouse in whose favour it was made applies for a divorce or an order under Part III of this Act.

(2) If the court does not discharge the order when it grants a divorce, it will remain in force and section 22 of this Act will apply to it.

Section 27

Amendment of the interpretation section of the Family Law (Maintenance of Spouses and Children) Act 1976.

Section 28

Orders for maintenance pending suit, periodical payments or secured periodical payments may be made through the District Court clerk, with any necessary modifications, including that:

    (a) the reference in section 9(4) of the 1976 Act to the "maintenance creditor" means the person to whom payments are to be made,

    (b) other references in Section 9 to the "maintenance creditor" refer to the person who applied for the order and

    (c) the reference in section 9(3) to the "maintenance debtor" means the person required to make payments under the order.

Section 29

The reference to "alimony" in the Defence Act 1954 includes orders for maintenance pending suit, periodical payments and secured periodical payments.

Section 30

Amendment of Enforcement of Court Orders Act 1940.

PART IV – INCOME TAX, CAPITAL ACQUISITIONS TAX, CAPITAL GAINS TAX, PROBATE TAX AND STAMP DUTY

Section 31

Payments under this Act (other than pensions) shall be made without deduction of income tax.

Section 32

Where a legally enforceable maintenance agreement is made

in a year of assessment by one spouse for the benefit of a divorced spouse and:

(a) both parties are resident in the state for tax purposes during that tax year and

(b) neither spouse has remarried,

then both spouses will be separately assessed for income tax, as if they had not been divorced.

Section 33

(1) Stamp duty will not be chargeable on a property transfer by either or both divorced spouses to either or both of them (See subsection (3))

(2) Section 74(2) of the Finance Act 1910 (on stamp duty payable on gifts from one person to another) shall not apply to such a transfer.

(3)(a) Subsection (1) applies to an order under Part III of this Act.

(b) Subsection (1) does not apply to any property transferred to anyone else.

Section 34

Any gift or inheritance that the court orders one spouse to give to the other shall be exempt from capital acquisitions tax and shall not be taken into account when computing such a tax.

Section 35

(1) If the court orders either spouse to dispose of an asset to the other spouse on divorce, both spouses shall be treated, for the purposes of capital gains tax, as if there were no loss or gain on the disposal. (This does not apply if the asset was part of the stock in the trade of the disposing spouse or if it is acquired as trading stock by the other spouse.)

(2) In the case of any subsequent disposal of the same asset, the spouse making the disposal will be treated (for capital gains tax purposes) as if the other spouse's acquisition

or provision of the asset was that of the disposing spouse.

Section 36

(1) Abatement or postponement of probate tax payable by a surviving spouse (under section 115A(1) of the Finance Act 1993) shall apply (with any necessary modifications) to:

    (a) a spouse who has been granted an order providing a benefit from the estate of his or her deceased former spouse and

    (b) any property interest which is the subject of such an order, in the same way as it applies to a person in s.115A who shares in the estate (or property interest) of a deceased spouse

PART V – MISCELLANEOUS

Section 37

(1) Interpretation section.

(2)(a) If proceedings have not been decided, the court may – on the application of the person bringing the proceedings–

    (i) restrain anyone from disposing of property or transferring it out of the state with the intention of defeating the applicant's claim

    (ii) set aside any disposition of property which has been disposed of to defeat the applicant's claim. (This does not apply to a property bought in good faith from a party to proceedings.) (See section 37(2)(c))

    (b) Where proceedings have been decided, if the court believes the other spouse (or anyone else) has disposed of property to defeat the applicant's claim, it may set aside the disposition.

    (c) An application under paragraph (a) shall be brought as part of the relevant proceedings.

(3) The court shall include in any order under subsection (2)(a) or (b) anything necessary for the order to be carried out, including the payment of money or disposition of any property.

(4) If the disposition of any property under subsection (2) took place less than three years before the application, or where the other spouse proposes to dispose of property and the court is satisfied that the disposition:

(a) would defeat, or

(b) has defeated

the applicant's claim, the court will presume (unless proved otherwise) that the intention was to defeat the claim.

Section 38

(1) The Circuit Family Court, as well as the High Court, may hear proceedings under this Act.

(2) Circuit Family Court proceedings relating to land with a rateable value of more than €254 must be transferred to the High Court on the application of anyone with an interest in the proceedings, but any order made by the Circuit Court before the transfer shall be valid unless the High Court decides otherwise. (See section 38(4))

(3) A Circuit Court judge may hear proceedings under this Act if any of the parties normally lives or works in the circuit area.

(4) If land has not been given a separate rateable valuation, the Circuit Court may decide its valuation.

(5) The Circuit Court shall hear proceedings under this Act in a different place (or different times or days) from other proceedings. Judges or lawyers will not wear wigs and gowns. The proceedings will be *in camera* and as informal as possible, consistent with the administration of justice.

(6) In proceedings under sections 13, 14, 15 (1)(a), 16, 17, 18 or 22,

(a) each spouse shall give the other spouse and anyone representing the interests of a dependent child and

(b) any dependent child shall give any other dependent child, anyone acting on behalf of such a child and each spouse

any details of property and income that may reasonably be required.

(7) If a person fails to give such details, the court may – on an application by anyone with an interest in the proceedings – direct compliance.

Section 39

(1) The court may only grant a decree of divorce if:
  (a) either spouse was domiciled in the state on the date the proceedings were instituted or
  (b) either spouse was ordinarily resident in the state for one year ending on that date.

(2) Where the court is hearing a divorce petition or appeal, it may grant a decree of judicial separation or nullity instead.

(3) Where the court is hearing a nullity petition or appeal, it may grant a decree of divorce instead.

(4) Where the court is hearing a judicial separation application or appeal, it may grant a decree of divorce instead.

Section 40

Anyone bringing proceedings under this Act must give notice to:
  (a) the other spouse(s) concerned, and
  (b) anyone else specified by the court.

Section 41

Where the court grants a divorce, it may declare that either of the parents is unfit to have custody of any dependent children under 18 and, if the other spouse dies, that parent shall not automatically have a right to the custody of those children.

Section 42
The court may order social reports from a probation officer, health board or anyone else.

Section 43
The cost of any mediation or counselling services for a spouse or dependent child under this Act or the 1989 Act, shall be at the discretion of the court.

Section 44
Where an engagement is broken off, the court will have power – as if the couple were married – to decide any dispute or claim to property in which either had an interest while they were engaged.

Section 45
Amendment of the Judicial Separation and Family Law Reform Act 1989.

Section 46
Amendment of the Succession Act 1965.

Section 47
Amendment of the Pensions Act 1990.

Section 48
Amendment of the Criminal Damage Act 1991.

Section 49
Amendment of the Criminal Evidence Act 1992.

Section 50
Amendment of the Powers of Attorney Act 1996.

Section 51
Amendment of the Domestic Violence Act 1996.

Section 52

Amendment of the Family Law Act 1995.

Section 53

Amendment of the Maintenance Act 1994 (as amended by the Family Law Act 1995).

(Note: "Dependent child" in this synopsis includes those in full-time education up to the age of 23 and those who are dependent by reason of physical or mental handicap. The words "he" and "she," or "husband" and "wife," are interchangeable.)

Appendix D

EC Family Law Regulation

Synopsis

Council Regulation (EC) No. 1347/2000 on jurisdiction and the recognition and enforcement of judgments in matrimonial matters and in matters of parental responsibility for children of both spouses came into force on March 1st 2001. (It does not apply in Denmark.)

This mandatory European Community law aims to ensure cross-border recognition of jurisdiction and judgments relating to the dissolution of marriage and parental responsibility for their children. The regulation also applies to nationals of non-Member States who have close links with a Member State.

The regulation deals with civil and non-judicial proceedings, and excludes purely religious procedures. It is confined to proceedings relating to divorce, legal separation, annulment, custody and access. The regulation does not cover issues such as the fault of spouses, property consequences of the marriage, maintenance or other ancillary measures.

The regulation covers parental responsibility for children of both spouses on any issues which are closely linked to proceedings for divorce, legal separation or nullity.

There must be a "real link" between the party concerned and the Member State exercising jurisdiction.

If one parent takes the child to another country, the fundamental interests of the children must be protected in accordance with the 1980 Hague Convention on the international abduction of children. "Habitual residence"

remains the basis of jurisdiction where there has been a *de
facto* change in residence because of the abduction.

This regulation does not prevent the courts of a Member
State from taking provisional measures in urgent cases with
regard to persons or property in that state.

The word "judgment" refers only to decisions that lead to
divorce, legal separation or nullity. Documents which have
been formally drawn up and are enforceable in one Member
State are equivalent to such judgments. Grounds for non-
recognition of judgments are kept to a minimum.

The State addressed should not review either the
jurisdiction of the State of origin nor the findings of fact. No
special procedures may be required for the updating of civil
status documents in one Member State on the basis of a final
judgment given in another Member State.

Article 1

1. This regulation applies to:
    (a) civil proceedings relating to divorce, legal separa-
         tion or marriage annulment;
    (b) civil proceedings relating to parental responsibility
         for the children of both spouses in those matrimonial
         proceedings.
2. Other proceedings officially recognised in a Member
State shall be regarded as equivalent to judicial proceedings.
The term "court" includes all authorities with jurisdiction in
these matters in the Member States.

3. The term "Member State" means all EU Member States
except Denmark.

Article 2

1. In matters relating to divorce, legal separation or

marriage annulment, jurisdiction shall lie with the courts of
the Member State:

    (a) in whose territory:
- the spouses are habitually resident, or
- the spouses were last habitually resident, insofar as one of them still lives there, or
- the respondent is habitually resident, or
- in the case of a joint application, either spouse is habitually resident, or
- the applicant is habitually resident if he or she lived there for at least a year immediately before the application was made, or
- the applicant is habitually resident if he or she lived there for at least six months immediately before the application was made and is either a national of the Member State in question or, in the case of the United Kingdom and Ireland, has a domicile there;

    (b) of the nationality of both spouses (or, in the case of Ireland and the United Kingdom, of the domicile of both spouses).

2. "Domicile" has the same meaning as it has under the legal systems of Ireland and the United Kingdom.

Article 3

1. Courts of a Member State exercising jurisdiction under Article 2 on an application for divorce, legal separation or marriage annulment shall have jurisdiction in matters of parental responsibility relating to a child of both spouses where the child is habitually resident in that Member State.

2. Where the child is not habitually resident in the Member State, the courts of that state shall have jurisdiction if the child is habitually resident in another Member State and

    (a) at least one of the spouses has parental responsibility

in relation to the child and
- (b) the jurisdiction of the courts has been accepted by the spouses and is in the best interests of the child.

3. The jurisdiction conferred by paragraphs 1 and 2 shall cease as soon as:
- (a) the judgment on the application for divorce, legal separation or annulment has become final or
- (b) where proceedings in relation to parental responsibility are still pending on the date referred to in (a), a judgment in these proceedings has become final; or
- (c) the proceedings referred to in (a) and (b) have come to an end for some other reason.

Article 4

Courts with jurisdiction under Article 3 shall exercise their jurisdiction in conformity with the Hague Convention, in particular Articles 3 and 16.

Article 5

The court in which proceedings are pending on the basis of Articles 2 to 4 also has jurisdiction to examine any counter-claim which comes within the scope of this regulation.

Article 6

Without prejudice to Article 2, a court of a Member State which has given a judgment on a legal separation shall also have jurisdiction to convert that judgment into a divorce, if the law of that state allows.

Article 7

A spouse who:

    (a) is habitually resident in the territory of a Member State or

    (b) is a national of a Member State (or, in the case of Ireland and the United Kingdom, is domiciled in the territory of one of those two Member States),

may be sued in another Member State only in accordance with Articles 2 to 6.

Article 8

1. Where no court of a Member State has jurisdiction pursuant to Articles 2 to 6, jurisdiction shall be decided in each Member State by the laws of that State.

2. Any national of a Member State who is habitually resident in another Member State may, like the nationals of that state, use the rules of jurisdiction in that state against a respondent who is not habitually resident and is not either a national of a Member State (or, in the case of Ireland and the United Kingdom, is not domiciled within the territory of one of those two Member States).

Article 9

A court shall declare that it has no jurisdiction in a matter in which the courts of another Member State have jurisdiction.

Article 10

1. Where a respondent habitually resident in a state other than the state where the action was brought does not enter an

appearance, the court with jurisdiction shall stay the proceedings, unless it is shown that the respondent received the
document instituting the proceedings in time to enable him
to arrange for his defence (or that all necessary steps had
been taken to this end).

2. Article 19 of Council Regulation (EC) No 1348/2000
on the service of documents applies instead of the provisions
of paragraph 1 of this article if the document instituting the
proceedings had to be sent from one Member State to another
under that regulation.

3. Where Regulation 1348/2000 is not applicable, Article
15 of the Hague Convention on the service of documents
abroad shall apply if the document had to be transmitted
abroad under that Convention.

Article 11

1. Where the same proceedings are brought before courts
of different Member States, the second court shall stay the
matter until the jurisdiction of the first court has been
established.

2. Where the proceedings involve the same parties but not
the same cause of action, the second court shall also stay
proceedings until the jurisdiction of the first court has been
established.

3. Where the first court has established jurisdiction, the
second court shall decline it and the person who brought the
action before the second court may take it before the first
court.

4. Proceedings are considered to be before a court:
  (a) when the document instituting the proceedings (or
      an equivalent document) is lodged with the court,
      provided that the applicant has not subsequently
      failed to take steps to effect service on the
      respondent or

(b) if the document has to be served before being lodged with the court, when it is received by the authority responsible for service, provided that the applicant has not subsequently failed to take steps to have the document lodged with the court.

Article 12

In urgent cases, this regulation shall not prevent the courts of one Member State from taking provisional, including protective, measures in respect of persons or assets in that state under the law of that State, even if the court of another Member State has jurisdiction over the substance of the matter.

Article 13

1. "Judgment" means a divorce, legal separation or marriage annulment granted by a court of a Member State, as well as a judgment relating to parental responsibility in such proceedings, whatever the judgment may be called, including a decree, order or decision.

2. This chapter also applies to the assessment of costs and to the enforcement of any costs or expenses order.

3. Documents which have been formally drawn up and are enforceable in one Member State, and settlements which have been approved by a court during proceedings and are enforceable in the state in which they were concluded, shall be enforceable under the same conditions as judgments.

Article 14

1. A judgment given in a Member State shall be recognised

in other Member States without the necessity for any special procedure.

2. In particular, no special procedure is required to update the civil records of a Member State on the basis of a final judgment relating to divorce, legal separation or marriage annulment given in another Member State.

3. Any interested party may apply for a decision that a judgment be (or not be) recognised.

4. Where the recognition of a judgment is raised incidentally in a court of a Member State, that court may determine that issue.

Article 15

1. A judgment relating to a divorce, legal separation or marriage annulment shall not be recognised:
   (a) if it is manifestly contrary to the public policy of the Member State in which recognition is sought;
   (b) where it was in default of appearance, if the respondent was not served with the document which instituted the proceedings (or with an equivalent document) in time to arrange for a defence, unless the respondent has accepted the judgment unequivocally;
   (c) if it is irreconcilable with a judgment given in proceedings between the same parties in the Member State in which recognition is sought or
   (d) if it is irreconcilable with an earlier judgment given between the same parties, provided that the earlier judgment fulfils the conditions necessary for recognition in that Member State.

2. A judgment relating to parental responsibility of spouses given during matrimonial proceedings shall not be recognised:
   (a) if it is manifestly contrary to the public policy of the Member State in which recognition is sought,

taking into account the best interests of the child;

(b) if it was given, except in urgent cases, without the child having had an opportunity to be heard, in violation of fundamental principles of procedure of the Member State in which recognition is sought;

(c) where it was given in default of appearance if the person in default was not served with the document which instituted the proceedings in time to arrange for a defence, unless the person has accepted the judgment unequivocally;

(d) at the request of any person claiming that the judgment infringes his or her parental responsibility, if that person had no opportunity to be heard;

(e) if it is irreconcilable with a later judgment in the Member State in which recognition is sought or

(f) if it is irreconcilable with a later judgment in another Member State or in the non-Member State of the habitual residence of the child, provided that the later judgment fulfils the conditions necessary for its recognition in the Member State in which recognition is sought.

Article 16

A court in a Member State may, on the basis of an agreement on the recognition and enforcement of judgments, refuse to recognise a judgment given in another Member State where, in cases set out in Article 8, the judgment could only be founded on grounds other than those set out in Articles 2 to 7.

Article 17

The jurisdiction of the court of the Member State of origin

may not be reviewed. The public policy test may not be applied to jurisdiction rules.

Article 18

Recognition of a judgment relating to divorce, legal separation or annulment may not be refused because the courts of the Member State in which such recognition is sought would not allow divorce, legal separation or marriage annulment on the same facts.

Article 19

The substance of a judgment may not be reviewed under any circumstances.

Article 20

1. A court of a Member State in which recognition is sought of a judgment given in another Member State may stay the proceedings if an ordinary appeal against the judgment has been lodged.

2. A court of a Member State in which recognition is sought of a judgment given in Ireland or the United Kingdom may stay the proceedings if enforcement has been suspended in Ireland or the UK because of an appeal.

Article 21

1. A judgment about parental responsibility for a child of both parties given in a Member State (which is enforceable in that Member State and has been served) shall be enforced

in another Member State when declared enforceable there on the application of any interested party.

2. In the United Kingdom, such a judgment shall be enforced in England and Wales, Scotland or Northern Ireland when it has been registered for enforcement in that part of the United Kingdom on the application of any interested party.

Article 22

1. An application for a declaration of enforceability shall be submitted to the court listed in Annex I.

2. The local jurisdiction shall be the place of the habitual residence of the person against whom enforcement is sought or the habitual residence of any child to whom the application relates. Where neither of these places is in the Member State where enforcement is sought, jurisdiction shall be decided by reference to the place of enforcement.

3. In relation to the procedures in Article 14(3), the local jurisdiction shall be determined by the internal law of the Member State in which proceedings are brought for recognition (or non-recognition).

Article 23

1. The application procedure shall be governed by the law of the Member State in which enforcement is sought.

2. The applicant must give an address for service within the jurisdiction of the court applied to. However, if the law of the Member State in which enforcement is sought does not provide for giving such an address, the applicant shall appoint a representative *ad litem*.

3. The documents referred to in Articles 32 and 33 shall be attached to the application.

Article 24

1. The court to which application has been made must give its decision without delay. The person against whom enforcement is sought shall not be entitled to make any submissions at this stage.

2. The application may be refused only for one of the reasons specified in Articles 15, 16 and 17.

3. The substance of a judgment may not be reviewed under any circumstances.

Article 25

The appropriate officer of the court shall bring the decision to the notice of the applicant without delay in accordance with procedures laid down by the law of the Member State in which enforcement is sought.

Article 26

1. Either party may appeal the decision on the application for a declaration of enforceability.

2. The appeal shall be lodged with the court listed in Annex II.

3. The appeal shall be dealt with according to the rules governing procedure in contested matters.

4. If the applicant brings an appeal for a declaration of enforceability, the party against whom enforcement is sought shall be summoned to appear before the appellate court. If such person fails to appear, the provisions of Article 10 apply.

5. An appeal must be lodged within one month of service thereof. If the party against whom enforcement is sought is habitually resident in a Member State other than that in which the declaration was given, the time for appealing shall be

two months and shall run from the date of service, on him or at his home. No extension may be granted on account of distance.

Article 27

A judgment given on appeal may be contested only by proceedings referred to in Annex III.

Article 28

1. The court with which the appeal is lodged under Articles 26 or 27 may, on the application of the party against whom enforcement is sought, stay the proceedings if an ordinary appeal has been lodged in the Member State of origin or if the time for such appeal has not yet expired. In the latter case, the court may specify the time within which an appeal is to be lodged.

2. Where the judgment was given in Ireland or the UK, any form of appeal available in the Member State of origin shall be treated as an ordinary appeal for the purposes of paragraph 1.

Article 29

1. Where a judgment has been given on several matters and enforcement cannot be authorised for all of them, the court shall authorise enforcement for one or more of them.

2. An applicant may request partial enforcement of a judgment.

Article 30

An applicant who received legal aid (or exemption from costs or expenses) in the Member State of origin is entitled, in procedures in Articles 22 to 25, to the most favourable legal aid (or most extensive exemption from costs and expenses) allowed by the law of the Member State addressed.

Article 31

No security, bond or deposit shall be required from anyone who applies for enforcement of a judgment given in another Member State on the grounds that:
- (a) he or she is not habitually resident in the Member State in which enforcement is sought; or
- (b) he or she is either a foreign national (or, where enforcement is sought in either the UK or Ireland, does not have his or her domicile in either of those Member States).

Article 32

1. A party seeking or contesting recognition or applying for a declaration of enforceability shall produce:
- (a) a copy of the judgment which satisfies the conditions to establish its authenticity, and
- (b) a certificate referred to in Article 33.

2. In the case of a default judgment, the party seeking recognition or applying for a declaration of enforceability shall also produce:
- (a) the original or certified true copy of the document which establishes that the defaulting party was served with the document instituting the proceedings (or with an equivalent document), or

(b) any document indicating that the defendant has accepted the judgment unequivocally.

Article 33

On the request of any interested party, the competent court or authority of a Member State where a judgment was given shall issue a certificate using the standard form in Annex IV (judgments in matrimonial matters) or Annex V (judgments on parental responsibility).

Article 34

1. If the documents specified in Article 32(1)(b) or (2) are not produced, the court may specify a time for their production, accept equivalent documents or, if it considers that it has sufficient information, dispense with their production.

2. A certified translation of such documents must be produced if the court requires.

Article 35

No legalisation or other similar formality shall be required in respect of the documents referred to in Articles 32, 33 and 34(2) or in respect of a document appointing a representative *ad litem*.

Article 36

1. This regulation supersedes other conventions between Member States relating to matters governed by this regulation.

2. Deals with matters relating to the Nordic States.

Article 37

This regulation shall take precedence over the 1961 Hague Convention on the law for protection of minors, the 1967 Luxembourg Convention on the recognition of decisions relating to the validity of marriages, the 1970 Hague Convention on the recognition of divorces and legal separations, the 1980 European Convention on the recognition and enforcement of decisions concerning child custody, the 1996 Hague Convention on jurisdiction in respect of parental responsibility and measures for the protection of children, provided that the child concerned is habitually resident in a Member State.

Article 38

1. The agreements and conventions referred to in Articles 36(1) and 37 shall continue to have effect in relation to matters to which this regulation does not apply.

2. They shall also continue to have effect in respect of judgments given and documents formally drawn up (or registered as authentic) before this regulation came into force.

Article 39

1. Member states may conclude agreements or arrangements to extend this regulation or to assist in its application. Member states shall send the Commission:

    (a) a copy of the draft agreements and

    (b) any denunciations of, or amendments to, these agreements.

2. In no circumstances may the agreements or arrangements derogate from Chapters II or III.

Article 40

Relates to concordats between Italy and Spain and the Vatican.

Article 41

In a state where two or more systems of law or sets of rules concerning matters governed by this regulation apply in different territories:

    (a) any reference to habitual residence in that Member State means habitual residence in a territorial unit;

    (b) any reference to nationality (or, in the case of the United Kingdom, domicile), means the territorial unit designated by the law of that state;

    (c) any reference to the authority of a Member State having received an application for divorce, legal separation or annulment means the authority of a territorial unit which has received such an application;

    (d) any reference to the rules of the requested Member State means the rules of the territorial unit in which jurisdiction, recognition or enforcement is invoked.

Article 42

This regulation applies only to legal proceedings instituted, documents formally drawn up and settlements approved by a court after March 1 2001. Judgments given in proceedings instituted before that date shall be recognised and enforced if jurisdiction was founded on rules which accorded with this regulation or on a convention between the two Member States when the proceedings were instituted.

This regulation is binding and directly applicable in the Member States in accordance with the Treaty establishing the European Community.

ANNEX I

The applications in Article 22 shall be submitted:
– in Ireland, to the High Court;
– in Northern Ireland, to the High Court of Justice;
– in England and Wales, to the High Court of Justice;
– in Scotland, to the Court of Session.

ANNEX II

The appeal in Article 26 shall be lodged:
– in Ireland, with the High Court;
– in Northern Ireland, with the High Court of Justice;
– in England and Wales, with the High Court of Justice;
– in Scotland, with the Court of Session.

ANNEX III

The appeals in Article 27 may be brought only:
– in Ireland, by an appeal on a point of law to the Supreme Court,
– in the United Kingdom, by a single further appeal on a point of law.

Appendix E

Legal Forms

Record No. 4567/2002

AN CHUIRT TEAGHLAIGH CHUARDA
(THE CIRCUIT FAMILY COURT)

DUBLIN CIRCUIT   **COUNTY OF DUBLIN**

IN THE MATTER OF THE FAMILY LAW
(DIVORCE) ACT 1996

Between/

CATHERINE O'BRIEN

Applicant

-and-

KENNETH O'BRIEN

Respondent

FAMILY LAW CIVIL BILL

YOU ARE HEREBY REQUIRED within ten days after the service of this civil bill upon you, to enter (or cause to be entered) with the registrar of the Circuit Family Court, at his office at Phoenix House, Smithfield, Dublin 7, an appearance to answer the claim of Catherine O'Brien of 1 Anglo Crescent, Ballinteer, in the County of the City of Dublin, the applicant herein as endorsed hereon.

AND TAKE NOTICE that, unless you do enter an appearance, you will be held to have admitted the said claim and the applicant may proceed therein and judgment given against you in your absence without further notice.

AND FURTHER TAKE NOTICE that if you intend to defend the proceedings on any grounds, you must not only enter an appearance as aforesaid, but also, within ten days after entry of the appearance, deliver a statement in writing showing the nature and grounds of your defence. The appearance and defence may be entered by posting them to the registrar's office and by sending copies to the applicant and her solicitor by post.

Dated 13 November, 2002

To: Kenneth O'Brien
The Mews,
Henderson Street,
Ballsbridge,
Dublin 4

Signed:_____
Arthur Smith & Co.,
Solicitor for the applicant

INDORSEMENT OF CLAIM

i   The applicant and respondent were married on 1 April 1990 at Sacred Heart Catholic Church, Morehampton Road, Donnybrook, in the City of Dublin.
ii   The applicant and respondent have been living apart for five years, since 2 April 1997. During that time the applicant lived at 1 Anglo Crescent, Ballinteer, in the County of the City of Dublin. The respondent lived at

The Mews, Henderson Street, Ballsbridge, Dublin 4.

iii   There are two dependent children of the marriage, namely Brendan born on 23 October 1990 and Vera born on 12 August 1993.

iv   The family home is 1 Anglo Crescent, Ballinteer, in the County of the City of Dublin, which the applicant and respondent own as joint tenants.

v   The family home is held by the respondent and applicant as joint tenants in fee simple.

vi   The applicant and respondent both live within the jurisdiction of this Honourable court. The rateable valuation of 1 Anglo Crescent, Ballinteer, is £22 (€27.93)

vii   The applicant is a nurse and the respondent is a hairdresser.

viii   At the date of institution of these proceedings, the applicant and respondent had lived apart from one another for at least four of the preceding five years. There is no reasonable prospect of any reconciliation between them. Proper provision, having regard to the circumstances, has been made for the respondent.

AND THE APPLICANT CLAIMS:

1. An order pursuant to s.5(1) of the 1996 Act for a decree of divorce.

2. An order pursuant to s.5(2) of the 1996 Act for directions concerning the dependent children's welfare, custody and access.

3. An order pursuant to s.11 of the 1996 Act for the custody, access or maintenance of the dependent children, before proceedings have been issued under the relevant Act.

4. An order pursuant to s.12(1) of the 1996 Act for the respondent to pay maintenance or a lump sum for the support of the applicant and dependent children from the date of the application until the date of the hearing.

5. An order pursuant to s.13(1) of the 1996 Act for
   (a) a periodical payments order,

    (b) a secured periodical payments order,
    (c) a lump sum payment.
6. An order pursuant to s.13(2) of the 1996 Act for payment of a lump sum to meet liabilities or expenses incurred before the application for a periodical payments order.
7. A property adjustment order pursuant to s.14(1) of the 1996 Act providing for the transfer by the respondent to the applicant of 1 Anglo Crescent, Ballinteer, in the County of City of Dublin.
8. An order pursuant to s.15(1)(a) of the 1996 Act
    (a) giving the applicant the right to live in the family home for life, to the exclusion of the respondent or
    (b) directing the sale of the family home and the division of the proceeds between the spouses.
9. An order pursuant to s.15(1)(c) of the 1996 Act dispensing with the consent of the respondent to the sale of the family home, protecting the home, relating to arrears of mortgage or rent or restricting the disposal of household chattels.
10. An order pursuant to s.18(10) of the 1996 Act that the respondent should not be entitled to provision out of the applicant's estate in the case of her death.
11. Any other order that may seem fitting to the court.
12. Costs.

AND FURTHER TAKE NOTICE that, in any cases where financial relief is sought by either party, you must file with the defence herein, or in any event within 20 days after the service of this civil bill upon you, at the aforementioned Circuit Court office, an affidavit of means (and, where appropriate, an affidavit of welfare) in the manner prescribed by the rules of this court, and serve a copy of same as provided by the rules of this court on the applicant or her solicitor at the address provided below.

Dated 13 November, 2002

Signed:_____

Arthur Smith & Co.,
Solicitor for the applicant,
342 College Green,
Dublin 2.

To: The Registrar,
Circuit Family Court,
Phoenix House,
Smithfield,
Dublin 7.

TAKE NOTICE that it is in your interest to have legal advice in regard to these proceedings. If you cannot afford a private solicitor, you may be entitled to legal aid provided by the state at a minimum cost to you. Details of this legal aid service are available at the Legal Aid Board, St Stephen's Green House, Dublin 2 (telephone 01-661 5811), where you can obtain the addresses and telephone numbers of the legal aid centres in your area.

Record No. 4567/2002

AN CHUIRT TEAGHLAIGH CHUARDA (THE CIRCUIT FAMILY COURT)

DUBLIN CIRCUIT   **COUNTY OF DUBLIN**

IN THE MATTER OF THE FAMILY LAW (DIVORCE) ACT 1996

Between/

CATHERINE O'BRIEN

Applicant

-and-

KENNETH O'BRIEN

Respondent

AFFIDAVIT OF MEANS

I, Catherine O'Brien of 1 Anglo Crescent, Ballinteer, in the County of the City of Dublin, nurse, aged 18 years and upwards, MAKE OATH and say as follows:

1. I am the applicant in the above-entitled proceedings and I make this affidavit of welfare from facts within my own knowledge, save where otherwise appears, and whereso appearing, I believe the same to be true.

2. I have set out in the first schedule hereto all the assets to which I am legally or beneficially entitled and the manner in which such property is held.

3. I have set out in the second schedule hereto all income which I have receive and the sources of such income.

4. I have set out in the third schedule hereto all my debts and/or liabilities and the persons to whom such debts and

liabilities are due.

5. My weekly outgoings amount to the sum of €669.60 and details of such outgoings have been set out in the fourth schedule hereto.

6. To the best of my knowledge, information and belief, all pension information known to me relevant to these proceedings is set out in the fifth schedule hereto (*or give reasons why the information has not been obtained*).

FIRST SCHEDULE

Assets

1. The property known as 1 Anglo Crescent, Ballinteer, in the County of the City of Dublin held in the joint names of the applicant and respondent and valued at €240,000
2. Savings   €520
3. Car   €6,500
4. Personal items   €1,000
5. Any other assets   Nil

SECOND SCHEDULE

Income

1. Salary   €37,000 per annum
2. Other income   €235 per month
3. Maintenance   €250 per week
4. Expenses   Nil

THIRD SCHEDULE

Debts and liabilities

1. Mortgage with Irish Permanent Building Society held
   jointly with the respondent   €110,000
2. Car loan with AIB Bank   €3,700

FOURTH SCHEDULE

Weekly personal outgoings

Mortgage	€197.00
Insurance (house, personal)	€17.50
House repairs and maintenance	€12.00
Food	€160.00
Car (tax, insurance, running costs)	€67.00
Fares	€8.00
TV/video rental	€6.50
Clothing	€35.00
Telephone	€26.00
Television licence/cable TV	€4.60
Oil, gas and electricity	€15.00
Family (birthdays, Christmas)	€16.00
Newspapers	€13.00
Holidays	€40.00
Medical, dental expenses	€26.00
Hairdresser	€6.00
Social	€20.00
Weekly total	€669.60

FIFTH SCHEDULE

Pension

The applicant is a member of the Department of Health pension scheme. An up-to-date pension statement is attached hereto.

> Sworn by the said Catherine
> O'Brien before me, a practising
> solicitor/Commissioner for
> Oaths, on (*date*)
> at (*address*)
> and I know the deponent.

Filed this ___ day of _____ 20__ by Arthur Smith & Co., solicitors for the applicant.

To: The Registrar,
Circuit Family Court,
Phoenix House,
Smithfield,
Dublin 7.

and

To: Kenneth O'Brien,
The Mews,
Henderson Street,
Ballsbridge,
Dublin 4

Record No. 4567/2002

AN CHUIRT TEAGHLAIGH CHUARDA
(THE CIRCUIT FAMILY COURT)

DUBLIN CIRCUIT   **COUNTY OF DUBLIN**

IN THE MATTER OF THE FAMILY LAW
(DIVORCE) ACT 1996

Between/

CATHERINE O'BRIEN

Applicant

-and-

KENNETH O'BRIEN

Respondent

AFFIDAVIT OF WELFARE

I, Catherine O'Brien of 1 Anglo Crescent, Ballinteer, in the County of the City of Dublin, nurse, aged 18 years and upwards, MAKE OATH and say as follows:
1. I am the applicant in the above-entitled proceedings and I make this affidavit of welfare from facts within my own knowledge, save where otherwise appears, and whereso appearing, I believe the same to be true.
2. I say and believe that the facts set out in the schedule hereto are true.

SCHEDULE

Part I – Details of the children

a. *Give details of the children born to (or adopted by) the respondent and applicant, with forenames, surnames and dates of birth.*
    Brendan O'Brien born on 23 October 1990, Vera O'Brien born on 12 August 1993.
b. *Give details of other children of the family, or children to whom either of the parties is* in loco parentis.
    None.

Part II – Arrangements for the children of the family – home details

a. *The address at which the children now live.*
    1 Anglo Crescent, Ballinteer, in the County of the City of Dublin.
b. *The number of living rooms, bedrooms at the above address(es).*
    2 living rooms, 3 bedrooms.
c. *Is the house rented or owned? Who is the tenant(s) or owner(s)?*
    Owned by the applicant and the respondent as joint tenant.
d. *Is the rent or mortgage being paid regularly? If so, by whom?*
    The mortgage is paid regularly by the applicant.
e. *Give the names of everyone else living with the chil-dren, full-time or part-time, and state their relationship to the children.*
    None.
f. *Will there be any changes to these arrangements? If so, give details.*
    No.

Part III – Education and training details

a. *Give details of the school, college or place of training attended by each child.*
   Brendan goes to Ballinteer CBS and Vera goes to Ballinteer Presentation.
b. *Do the children have special educational needs? If so, specify in detail.*
   No.
c. *Is the school, college or place of training fee-paying? If so, how much are the fees per term or year? Are the fees paid regularly and, if so, by whom?*
   Not fee-paying.
d. *Will there be any changes in these circumstances? If so, give details.*
   No.

Part IV – Childcare details

a. *Which parent looks after the children from day to day? If responsibility is shared, give details.*
   The applicant.
b. *Give details of the work commitments of both parents.*
   Both forty hours per week during normal business.
c. *Does someone look after the children when the parents are not there? If so, give details.*
   Professional childminder and/or applicant's mother.
d. *Who looks after the children during school holidays?*
   Professional childminder and/or applicant's mother.
e. *Will there be any changes to these arrangements? If so, give details.*
   No.

Part V – Maintenance

a. *Does the respondent pay towards the upkeep of the children? If so, give details. Specify any other sources of maintenance.*
   Yes – €150 per week. The respondent also pays €100 a week maintenance for the applicant.
b. *Is this maintenance paid under court order? If so, give details.*
   No.
c. *Has maintenance been agreed for the children? If so, give details.*
   Yes – €150 per week.
d. *Will you be applying for a maintenance order from the court?*
   Yes.

Part VI – Details of contact with children

a. *Do the children see the respondent? Give details.*
   Yes – access at his home from 8am on Saturday until 10am on Sunday every week.
b. *Do the children stay overnight and/or have holiday visits with the respondent? Give details.*
   Yes – see above and holiday access during July and/or August for two consecutive weeks, subject to three weeks' advance notice in writing to the applicant. Also access during all three days up to and including Christmas Day and Easter Sunday and access from 6pm to 8pm on the birthday of each child.
c. *Will there be any changes to these arrangements? If so, give details.*
   No.

Part VII – Details of health

a. *Are the children generally in good health? Detail any serious disability or chronic illness suffered by any of the children.*
Yes.

b. *Do any of the children have any special health needs? Give details of care needed and how it is to be provided.*
No.

c. *Are the applicant or respondent generally in good health? If not, give details.*
Yes.

Part VIII – Details of care and other court proceedings

a *Is any of the children in the care of a health board or under the supervision of a social worker or probation officer? If so, give details.*
No.

b. *Have there been any court proceedings involving any of the children? If so, give details. (All relevant court orders should be annexed.)*
No.

Sworn by the said Catherine
O'Brien before me, a practising
solicitor/Commissioner for
Oaths, on (*date*)
at (*address*)
and I know the deponent.

Filed this ___ day of _____20__by Arthur
Smith & Co., solicitors for the applicant.

To: The Registrar,
Circuit Family Court,
Phoenix House,
Smithfield,
Dublin 7.

and

To: Kenneth O'Brien,
Henderson Street,
Ballsbridge,
Dublin 4.

Record No. 4567/2002

AN CHUIRT TEAGHLAIGH CHUARDA (THE CIRCUIT FAMILY COURT)

DUBLIN CIRCUIT   **COUNTY OF DUBLIN**

IN THE MATTER OF THE FAMILY LAW (DIVORCE) ACT 1996

Between/

CATHERINE O'BRIEN

Applicant

-and-

KENNETH O'BRIEN

Respondent

CERTIFICATE PURSUANT TO SECTION 6 OF THE FAMILY LAW (DIVORCE) ACT 1996

I, Arthur Smith, the solicitor acting for the above-named applicant, hereby certify as follows:

1. I have discussed with the applicant the possibility of reconciliation with the respondent and I have given the applicant the names and addresses of persons qualified to help effect a reconciliation between spouses who have become estranged.
2. I have discussed with the applicant the possibility of engaging in mediation to help effect a divorce on a basis agreed between the applicant and the respondent, and I have given the applicant the names and addresses of persons qualified to provide a mediation service for

spouses who have become estranged.
3   I have ensured that the applicant is aware of judicial
separation/separation agreement as an alternative to
divorce, no decree of judicial separation in relation to the
applicant and the respondent being in force.

Dated 13 November, 2002

Signed:_____
Arthur Smith & Co.,
Solicitors,
342 College Green,
Dublin 2.

Record No. 4567/2002

AN CHUIRT TEAGHLAIGH CHUARDA
(THE CIRCUIT FAMILY COURT)

DUBLIN CIRCUIT   **COUNTY OF DUBLIN**

IN THE MATTER OF THE FAMILY LAW
(DIVORCE) ACT 1996

Between/

CATHERINE O'BRIEN

Applicant

-and-

KENNETH O'BRIEN

Respondent

DEFENCE AND COUNTERCLAIM

TAKE NOTICE that the respondent, Kenneth O'Brien, of The Mews, Henderson Street, Ballsbridge, Dublin 4, disputes the claims made in the applicant's family law civil bill pursuant to sections 11, 12(1), 13(1), 13(2), 14(1), 15(1)(a), 15(1)(c), 18(10), of the 1996 Act, which was served on the respondent on 13 November, 2002.

AND FURTHER TAKE NOTICE that the respondent will rely on the following matters in disputing the applicant's claim:

i   The respondent admits paragraphs (i) to (viii) in the civil bill, but denies that proper provision has been made for the respondent.

COUNTERCLAIM

AND TAKE NOTICE that the respondent will rely on the following matters in support of his counterclaim:

1. The respondent repeats his answer herein.
2. The respondent and the applicant were lawfully married on 1 April 1990 at Sacred Heart Catholic Church, Morehampton Road, Donnybrook, in the City of Dublin .
3. The respondent and applicant are, and were at the date of the said ceremony, domiciled in Ireland and are ordinarily resident within the jurisdiction of this court.
4. The respondent and applicant have been living apart since 2 April 1997 and there is no reasonable prospect of reconciliation between them. Proper provision has been made for the applicant herein.
5. There are two dependent children of the marriage, namely Brendan O'Brien born on 23 October 1990 and Vera O'Brien born on 12 August 1993.
6. The family home is situated at 1 Anglo Crescent, Ballinteer, in the County of the City of Dublin, and is held in the joint names of the respondent and the applicant. The value of the property is approximately €240,000. There is an outstanding loan on the property in the amount of €110,000. The rateable value of the property is £22 (€27.93)

AND THE RESPONDENT CLAIMS:

1. An order pursuant to s.5(1) of the 1996 Act for a decree of divorce.
2. An order pursuant to s.5(2) of the 1996 Act for directions concerning the dependent children's welfare, custody and access.
3. An order pursuant to s.11 of the 1996 Act for the custody, access or maintenance of a dependent child, before

proceedings have been issued under the relevant Act.

4. An order pursuant to s.14 (1) of the 1996 Act for a property adjustment order providing for the transfer of 1 Anglo Crescent, Ballinteer, in the County of the City of Dublin, by the applicant to the respondent.

5. An order pursuant to s.15(1)(e) of the 1996 Act for the partition of property.

6. An order pursuant to s.15(1)(f) of the 1996 Act for custody or access or relating to the welfare of a child.

7. An order pursuant to s.19(1) of the 1996 Act for the sale of property in which either spouse has an interest.

8. Any other order that may seem fitting to the court.

9. Costs.

Dated 20 November 2002

Signed:_____
Diana Goodbody,
Solicitor for the respondent
642 Dame Street,
Dublin 2.

To: The Registrar,
Circuit Family Court,
Phoenix House,
Smithfield,
Dublin 7.

And to: Arthur Smith & Co.,
Applicant's solicitor
342 College Green,
Dublin 2.

SAMPLE SEPARATION AGREEMENT

This separation agreement made on the 4th of May 2003 between Catherine O'Brien of 1 Anglo Crescent, Ballinteer, in the County of the City of Dublin, (hereinafter called "the wife") and Kenneth O'Brien of The Mews, Henderson Street, Ballsbridge, Dublin 4, (hereinafter called "the husband"):

WHEREAS

1. The husband and the wife were married to one another on the 1st of April 1990 at Sacred Heart Catholic Church, Morehampton Road, Donnybrook, in the City of Dublin.
2. There are two living children of the marriage, (hereinafter called "the children") namely Brendan, born on the 23rd day of October 1990 and Vera, born on the 12th day of August 1993.
3. The husband and wife have been living apart from each other since April 2nd 2001.

The parties have AGREED that, while living apart, the following provisions shall have effect and regulate their mutual rights and obligations:

1. The husband and wife shall live separate and apart from and free from the marital control of the other and neither the husband nor the wife shall in any manner annoy, disturb, molest or otherwise interfere with the other's manner of living, profession, business, friends, relations or acquaintances, nor use any force, violence or restraint on the other, with the intent that each shall live henceforth as if he or she were sole and unmarried.
2. Neither the husband nor the wife shall visit or be or stay in any place in which the other is for the time being resident, without the express invitation of the other.
3. The husband and wife shall remain joint guardians of the

children. The wife shall have sole custody and the husband shall have such access to the children as may be from time to time agreed, including access at his home from 8am on Saturday until 10am on Sunday every week, and holiday access during July and/or August for two consecutive weeks, subject to three weeks' advance notice in writing to the wife. The husband shall also have access during all three days up to and including Easter Sunday and Christmas Day and access from 6pm to 8pm on the birthday of each child.

4. The husband and wife agree that they will consult each other as far as possible on matters affecting the children's upbringing, education, training, medical care and general welfare, and that they will immediately notify the other if either of the children should require the services of a doctor. The parent having care and control of the children at that time shall be absolutely entitled to obtain and provide such medical care, including hospitalisation and any medical or surgical treatment, as may be necessary. The husband and wife agree that both will receive copies of any school reports and both shall be entitled to attend parent-teacher meetings at the children's school.

5. Neither parent shall remove either child outside the jurisdiction of the courts of the Republic of Ireland without the prior written consent of the other, such consent not to be unreasonably withheld. The wife shall have custody of the children's passports.

6. Each parent shall refrain from interfering with or diminishing the love, affection and respect of the children for the other parent and shall not do or say or omit to do or say anything which would tend to lower the other parent in the esteem of either of the children. Neither parent shall interfere with reasonable communication by telephone or post between either of the children and the other parent.

7. The husband and wife hereby agree to the following financial arrangements for the foreseeable future:

(a) That the husband will pay to the wife the sum of €250 per week for the support of the wife and the children, being €100 for the wife and €75 for each child. The first payment shall be made on May 9 2003 and payments thereafter shall be made weekly on each subsequent Friday into the wife's building society account number 016794477 at Bank of Ireland, Grafton Street, Dublin 2.

(b) The maintenance payable by the husband shall be reviewed annually in the first week of January and shall be varied by a percentage either in accordance with the latest consumer price index published by the Central Statistics Office for the previous 12 months or in accordance with any variation in the husband's net income during the preceding tax year, whichever is the lesser, and such varied sum shall become due and payable to the wife weekly from the following Friday in the manner set out in clause 7(a) hereof.

(c) The maintenance payable for each child shall cease to be paid upon that child attaining the age of 18 years or, if still attending at a full-time course at any university, college, school or educational institute, until the child attains the age of 23 years or completes full-time education, whichever is the earlier. Maintenance in respect of either of the children shall also cease in the event of the death of that child.

(d) In the event of a significant change in the financial circumstances of either the husband or the wife, either party may serve notice on the other of an intention to seek an increase or decrease in the amount of maintenance payable under this agreement and specifying the amount of main-tenance considered reasonable in the altered circumstances. On the service of such notice, both

parties shall make available to the other within four
weeks full details of his or her financial circumstances. If agreement is not reached on a revised
sum of maintenance within four weeks of the receipt
of such details, the parties agree to accept the
decision of an arbitrator appointed by the chairman
of the Bar Council as to the sum payable thereafter.

(e) The wife shall be entitled to continue to receive all
social welfare benefits in respect of the children.

(f) The husband agrees to continue paying a monthly
premium of €40 on the life assurance policy number
8172783 held with the Coach House Insurance
Company and agrees that the wife shall continue to
be the named beneficiary thereon.

(g) Maintenance payments shall cease in the event of
any of the following:
  (i)   the death of the husband,
  (ii) the death of the wife,
  (iii) the wife going through a ceremony of marriage
        with another person at any time,
  (iv) the wife cohabiting with another person as if
        they were husband and wife for a continuous
        period of at least three months,
  (v)   the court making a maintenance order which
        supersedes this agreement,
  (vi) the court granting a decree of nullity to the
        husband or wife.

8. In the event of the marriage of the parties hereto being
    dissolved by a decree of divorce, any property purchased
    or money saved by the wife out of maintenance payments
    made to her by the husband shall belong solely to the
    wife, and the husband shall have no interest or claim
    therein and Section 21 of the Family Law (Maintenance
    of Spouses and Children) Act 1976 shall not apply thereto

9. The husband and wife shall be separately assessed for
    income tax pursuant to Section 3 of the Finance Act 1983

and shall be treated as single persons in the future for all tax purposes.

10. The husband acknowledges that the household chattels at present remaining in the family home are and will remain the sole property of the wife.

11. The husband hereby agrees to assure to the wife the beneficial ownership of all his estate and interest in the family home situate at 1 Anglo Crescent, Ballinteer, in the County of the City of Dublin, free from encumbrances save the mortgage next referred, freed and discharged from all claims which he may have in respect of the same, whether under the Family Home Protection Act 1976 or otherwise, and the wife hereby agrees that in consideration of such assurances, she will indemnify and keep indemnified the husband from and against all claims arising hereafter on foot of the building society mortgage at present secured on the family home and the husband shall, prior to the execution of this agreement, deliver to the wife such deed of assurance and at any time thereafter, at the request of the wife or any person acting on her behalf, shall execute such deed, document or consent as may be required for the purpose of sale or otherwise for the purpose of giving full legal effect to this agreement.

12. The wife hereby agrees with the husband that she will at all times in the future support and maintain herself and the children out of the maintenance payments made by the husband pursuant to this agreement, together with any income received by her from any other source, and the husband and the wife agree that they will at all times keep the other indemnified from all debts and liabilities heretofore or hereafter contracted howsoever arising, and from all actions, costs, claims, damages, demands, losses and expenses in respect of any such debts or liabilities.

13. The husband and the wife hereby mutually surrender and renounce all succession rights due to either of them under the provisions of the Succession Act 1965 or any share

or legal right in the estate of the other at any time, provided that either of them may take any legal action necessary to protect or defend the interests of the children in the estate of either the husband or the wife.

14. The husband shall pay the wife's costs in connection with the preparation, drafting and execution of this agreement, to be taxed in default of agreement on a solicitor/client basis.

15. The husband and wife agree that this agreement shall not be regarded as an approbation or ratification of a void or voidable marriage.

16. The husband and wife hereby agree for all purposes that this agreement is in full and final settlement of all present and future financial and property claims (save for periodic maintenance) which either shall have against the other under the Constitution of Ireland 1937, the Married Women's Status Act 1957, the Family Law (Maintenance of Spouses and Children) Act 1976, the Judicial Separation and Family Law Reform Act 1989, the Family Law Act 1995, the Family Law (Divorce) Act 1996 or any amending Act of the Oireachtas or under similar legislation in this or any other jurisdiction, under the rules of equity or the common law or otherwise. The parties agree not to issue or maintain proceedings under any legislative provisions in this clause, save in respect of periodic maintenance.

IN WITNESS WHEREOF the parties hereto have hereunto set their hands and affixed their seals on the day and year first herein written

Signed, sealed and delivered by the said Kenneth O'Brien

Kenneth O'Brien

in the presence of:

> *Diana Goodbody*

Signed, sealed and delivered by the said Catherine O'Brien

> *Catherine O'Brien*

in the presence of:

> *Arthur Smith*

JOINT GUARDIANSHIP DECLARATION

The mother and father of a non-marital child must both make this statutory declaration if they wish the father to become a guardian of the child jointly with the mother. If there is more than one child, a separate statutory declaration should be made for each.

If the parents of the child cannot agree about the father's appointment as joint guardian, the father can apply to the court to be made a joint guardian under section 6A of the Guardianship of Infants Act 1964.

A father who is appointed guardian by this joint statutory declaration can only be removed as guardian by court order.

Guardianship is the collection of rights and duties of a parent towards a child. It includes the duty to maintain and properly care for the child, as well as the right to make decisions about a child's religious and secular education, health requirements and other matters affecting the child's welfare. The exercise of guardianship rights may be agreed between parents. If they disagree about the exercise of these rights, either parental guardian may ask the court to decide the matter.

The right to custody is one of the rights that arises under the guardianship relationship. Custody is the physical day-to-day care and control of a child. Even where one parental guardian has custody of a child, the other parental guardian is generally entitled to be consulted about matters affecting the child's welfare.

A father's duty to maintain his child and his right to apply to the court for custody or access to his child does not depend on his being made a guardian.

The appointment of a natural father as guardian will affect any adoption of the child. A child ceases to be subject to guardianship when he reaches the age of 18 or marries.

This declaration will seriously affect the legal position of both parents and it is advisable to obtain legal advice before making it. This is an important document and should be kept in a safe place when completed.

In the matter of a declaration
under paragraph (e) of section 2(4) (inserted by the
Children Act, 1997) of the Guardianship of Infants Act
1964.

We

_____ (*father's name*)

of _____ (*father's address*)

and

_____ (*mother's name*)

of _____ (*mother's address*)

do solemnly and sincerely declare and say as follows:

1. We have not married each other.

2. We are the father and mother of _____ (*child's name*) who was born on the____day of _____ 200 _____.

3. We agree to the appointment of _____(*father's name*) as a guardian of _____ (*child's name*)

4. We have entered into arrangements regarding the custody of [and access to] * _____ (*child's name*) [*Strike out as necessary*]

We make this solemn declaration conscientiously believing the same to be true by virtue of the Statutory Declarations Act 1938 and pursuant to paragraph (e) of section 2(4) (inserted by the Children Act, 1997) of the Guardianship of Infants Act 1964.

Signed _____ (*father*)

Signed _____ (*mother*)

Declared before me by

_____ (*father's name*)

and _____ (*mother's name*)

who are personally known to me (or who are identified to me by

_____ who is personally known to me)

at _____

on this _____ day of _____ 20_____.

(Signature of practising solicitor/Peace Commissioner/ Commissioner for Oaths/Notary Public)

Appendix F

Useful Contacts

Legal

Legal Aid Board
4th Floor, St. Stephen's Green House,
Earlsfort Terrace, Dublin 2
www.legalaidboard.ie
legalaidboard@eircom.net
Tel: 01-661 5811

Free Legal Advice Centres
49 South William Street, Dublin 2
www.flac.ie
flac@connect.ie
Tel: 01-679 4239

Incorporated Law Society (solicitors)
Blackhall Place, Dublin 7
www.lawsociety.ie
general@lawsociety.ie
Tel: 01-671 0711

Law Library (barristers)
Four Courts, Inns Quay, Dublin 7
www.lawlibrary.ie
barcounsel@lawlibrary.ie
Tel: 01-872 0622

Conciliation and Mediation

Accord (Catholic marriage counselling)
Columba Centre, Maynooth, Co. Kildare
www.accord.ie
admin@accord.ie
Tel: 01-505 3112

Marriage and Relationship Counselling Services
24 Grafton Street, Dublin 2
mrcs@eircom.net
Tel: 01-679 9341

Aim Family Services
6 D'Olier Street, Dublin 2
www.aimfamilyservices.ie
aimfamilyservices@eircom.net
Tel: 01-670 8363

Clanwilliam Institute
18 Clanwilliam Terrace, Grand Canal Quay, Dublin 2
www.clanwilliam.ie
office@clanwilliam.ie
Tel: 01-676 1363

Family Therapy and Counselling
46 Elmwood Avenue Lower, Ranelagh, Dublin 6
ftcc@eircom.net
Tel: 01-497 1188

Turning Point
23 Crofton Road, Dun Laoghaire, Co. Dublin
turningpoint@eircom.net
Tel: 01-280 7888

Al-Anon
5 Capel Street, Dublin 1
Tel: 01-873 2699

Samaritans
112 Marlborough Street, Dublin 1
jo@samaritans.org
Tel: 01-872 7700

Bereavement Counselling Service
St Ann's Church, Dawson Street, Dublin 2
Tel: 01-676 7727

Mediators' Institute of Ireland
72 Beechpark Road, Foxrock, Dublin 18
www.mediatorsinstituteireland.ie
info@mediatorsinstituteireland.ie
Tel: 01-661 8488

Family Mediation Service
1st Floor, St Stephen's Green House,
Earlsfort Terrace, Dublin 2
commsupport.welfare.ie/foi/fms_foi.xml
fmsearlsfort@oceanfree.net
Tel: 01-634 4320

Parents and children

Gingerbread (single parents)
Carmichael Centre, North Brunswick Street, Dublin 7
www.gingerbread.ie
info@gingerbread.ie
Tel: 01-814 6618

ISPCC
20 Molesworth Street, Dublin 2
www.ispcc.ie
ispcc@ispcc.ie
Tel: 01-679 4944

Deserted Husbands' Association
54 Foster Terrace, Ballybough, Dublin 3
Tel: 01-855 2334

Separated Persons' Association
Carmichael House, North Brunswick Street, Dublin 7
Tel: 01-872 0684

Parental Equality
54 Middle Abbey Street, Dublin 1
www.parentalequality.ie
info@parentalequality.ie
Tel: 01-872 5222

Amen
9/10 Academy Street, Navan, Co Meath
www.amen.ie
Tel: 046-23718

Minus One
68 Lower Leeson Street, Dublin 2

Parentline (parents under stress)
Carmichael House, North Brunswick Street, Dublin 7
www.parentline.ie
parentline@eircom.net
Helpline: 01-873 3500
Office: 01-878 7230

Cura (unwanted pregnancy)
30 South Anne Street, Dublin 2
Tel: 01-671 0598

Adoption Board
Shelbourne House, Shelbourne Road, Ballsbridge, Dublin 4
www.adoptionboard.ie
Tel: 01-667 1392

Women's Aid
Everton House, 47 Old Cabra Road, Dublin 7
Helpline 1800 341 900
www.womensaid.ie
info@womensaid.ie
Tel: 01-868 4721

Society of St Vincent de Paul
8 New Cabra Road, Phibsboro, Dublin 7
www.svp.ie
info@svp.ie
Tel: 01-838 4164
www.solo.ie Irish website supporting lone parents

Treoir
Information Centre for Unmarried Parents
14 Gandon House,
Lower Mayor Street, IFSC, Dublin 1
Tel: 01-670 0120
indigo.ie/~treoir

Marriage

Dublin Catholic Marriage Tribunal
Archbishop's House, Drumcondra, Dublin 9
Tel: 01-837 9253

Registrar of Civil Marriages (Dublin)
Sir Patrick Duns Hospital, Lr. Grand Canal Street, Dublin 2
Tel: 01-678 7114

Registrar General
Joyce House, 8/11 Lombard Street, Dublin 2
www.groireland.ie
Dublin Tel: 01-671 1929/1968/1974
Country section Tel: 01-671 1000

UK Divorce Registry
First Avenue House, 42–49 High Holborn, London, WC1V 6NP
Tel: 0044-207 947 600

Index